THE TREE CLIMBERS

A CHILDHOOD IN WAR TIME BRIGHTON.

BY
DAVID J. KNOWLES.

PUBLISHED BY
KNOWLES PUBLISHING
ROCHESTER.

FIRST PUBLISHED 1998
KNOWLES PUBLISHING. ROCHESTER.

IBSN 09534358 0 6

The cover photograph is an aerial photograph of Sussex Square - Lewes Crescent and the gardens probably taken in the 1930's

Cover design Redwood books.

Published by Knowles publishing
18   Castle Av. Rochester. Kent.

Printed by Redwood Books.Trowbridge

DEDICATION.

For my wife Pamela - without whom this book wouldn't have got off the ground - and in memory of my mother and father, who like so many other parents, had the daunting 'duty' of bringing up children during those long, austere and quite often frightening war years.

ACKNOWLEDGEMENTS.

My thanks also go to all the following:-

Dr.Douglas Flowers, for all his keen interest and time spent getting me very helpful photostats.   Brighton reference library - a mine of information.   The Evening Argus for allowing me to use some of their wartime reports.
Robert Boddie, Librarian Sussex County Cricket Club - for so much help concerning my great uncle W.L.Knowles.   Also Mr.C.H.Taylor, Kent C.C.C. for further information about this cricketing relative. Captain Penny, Lake Superior Regiment. Canada. For permission to quote from 'In the Face of Danger' by Lieut.Col.George F. Stanley. Christopher Apps Brighton College Junior School archivist. Jean Roberts St.Mary's Hall archivist for so much time, and for bringing a lot of valuable information to light.   Mr.C.W.Wilson, Wilson's laundry Arundel Road, Brighton - for some fascinating bits of information.
Imperial War Museum.   Ministry of Agriculture and Fisheries. for their extensive details on wartime rationing.   B.B.C. Resources, Reading for information about Bruce Belfrage. National Railway Museum, York.   East Sussex records office Lewes.

Mr.J.G.Davies, Ovingdean historian, for information from 'A Potted History Of The Lands Of Ovingdean'.   St.Dunstans, for some lines from - 'St.Dunstans a Story of Accomplishment'. Dulcie Carnaghan (nee Filkins and great granddaughter of Henry Cowley of Ovingdean) for information and a picture of the Grange as it was in the thirties and forties.   Jonathan Rolls, estate agent. Brighton. Alan Ashwell, Kemptown Enclosures. 'Leave It To Jeeves' Bighton Marina.   The London Weather Centre.

Also - in the family - my sister Jill for always being just a phone call away to answer a multitude of questions. My eldest son Paul, for help with the photographs, my youngest son Timothy for the computer work and type setting and teaching his mother some of the intricacies of this 'strange world' of computers, and my other son Mark for keeping on phoning me from up north and telling me "to get on with it!"   For Sylvia, my stepmother for the reading and the corrections and dedication and for Mary Buck our very good friend for all her reading.

Also, many thanks to everyone who helped and are not mentioned here, for the information, the hints, the ideas - and most of all - the encouragement.

CONTENTS.

ILLUSTRATIONS

FORWARD.

At first there was the very real threat of invasion – then came the
air raids, including the Battle of Britain - many
of the 'dog fights, were fought in the skies over Brighton. There
was the dilemma for the schools - should they stay
as they were - evacuate - or close down?   There was also
the humour and determination.   Perhaps most importantly
there was that feeling of everyone being in the same boat
thereby helping to bond communities together.
This is the story of those traumatic war years in the 'restricted'
town of Brighton - it is the story of a time that
will remain in the history books - a time for many of us which is
unforgettable.

THE TREE CLIMBERS.

CHAPTER ONE.

Sussex Square Gardens. – It's War – The Ice Storm.

Until that Sunday morning, all the talk about a war coming, hadn't really affected us children who made up a small group who usually always played together in the gardens. We had heard all the talk of course, and perhaps understood some of it, we had listened or overheard, while bits and pieces had been read out from the newspapers by our parents, and now and again also listened to odds and ends on the wireless, without really taking them in; after all, there were more important things to occupy our minds, and the gardens were the centre of where we imaginatively created our varying activities during the long summer days.

We lived in Sussex Square, a beautiful Regency built part of Brighton at the easterly end of the area known as Kemptown, and the gardens lie between the square and its close neighbours - the east and west sides of Lewes Crescent. There are the top gardens, which lie completely within the square, then comes the Eastern Road - where the town buses run past, and then, the much larger bottom gardens which stretch down to the main coastal road. After that come the grass slopes that lead down to Madeira Drive, nearby which, Volks Railway makes its rickety journey between the Palace Pier and what is now the Marina, but which used to be Black Rock bathing pool and the beginning of the undercliff walk to Ovingdean, Rottingdean and Saltdean. Beyond this old electric railway are the beaches, and then, apart from any boats, an uninterrupted view of the channel to the horizon.

The gardens are exclusive to the residents of the square and crescents that entwine them, and an annual fee entitles you to your own key.   There is a tunnel which runs between the bottom gardens and the slopes, that goes under the main coastal road, and you also need your key to use this short cut to the beaches.

My grandparents, on my mothers side of the family, had bought number thirteen Sussex Square in the early 1920s, and at first my parents had lived in the top flat;   in 1929 my sister Jill was born there and I also made my entry into the world there in the April of 1933.

My father was a retired ex-regular army officer.   In the First World War he had been wounded at the Battle of Mons, so, at the end of that war, he took retirement because of his wounds, eventually becoming a representative for a Brighton firm of builders merchants.   He had a two seater car with a tiny compartment in the back that was just big enough for Jill and me to squeeze into, for trips into the countryside.   He now missed the army very much, and with the likelihood of another war just around the corner, he felt very frustrated that he wouldn't be a part of the action again - in what he thought would be a necessary war against a desperate evil.   From time to time, if we had guests for dinner, the Battle of Mons would be fought all over again; typifying the scene where the port becomes the thin red line of the British; the nuts - the German army, and the pineapple - where my father was!   Some people still called him "captain," but to their friends, our parents were just - Lance and Doris.

In 1937 the shrapnel still remaining in his leg became gangrenous, and during a life threatening illness, the leg was amputated from well above the knee, and although he had lost a leg, he, and the surgeon commander of the army officers hospital in Percival Terrace in Brighton - 'Major John Murdoch' - had won the battle for his life, very ably assisted by the nursing staff of nuns. He now walked with the help of a stump type of false leg - one which clicks down at the knee when you sit down.   The leg had been cut off from too high up for him to successfully and comfortably wear a proper false limb.   This had also made it practically impossible to get up and down all the stairs at number thirteen - there was no lift there.   Fortunately the ground floor flat had recently become vacant, and, shortly after he had come out of hospital, we moved into that.

On that particular Sunday morning in 1939, I could sense it was going to be a different sort of day.   To start with my mother had made no mention of going to church, when she did go - she usually insisted I accompany her - sometimes   Jill came too, but more often than not it was just me - my father never came.   Also I had noticed from the window that Peter had already arrived in the gardens, and a few minutes later Janine arrived there too, this was early for her, and me, but when I asked my mother if I could join them, she agreed straight away.   Michael arrived at the same time as me, and the four of us had the gardens to ourselves - except for Ham, the head gardener, who was strolling round inspecting the plants and things; it was supposed to be his day off, so we were a little puzzled at his being there.   I had been told that there was going to be an important announcement by the Prime Minister on the wireless that morning, and apparently, after that, we would know if there was going to be a war or not.   We sat on the grass and talked for a while, and when we heard a gate shutting and saw Ham crossing the road and obviously on his way home, we felt that it would be alright now to climb our favourite tree, which although tall, was easy for us to climb, with the main branches not far apart. Michael and I went first and quite quickly reached the branches we called 'our special camp,' close to the top of the tree. This was the second largest of the four fir trees which stood at the four corners of the top gardens. Peter followed, with Janine just a little way behind him - they stopped several feet below us, with Janine sitting on a thick branch a little below Peter. "Come on Jan," I called out, "try and get up here". She had never climbed that far before, but often said she would do next time.   "I can't get round Peter - he's too fat !"   Janine quickly excused herself.   Michael and I simultaneously glanced down at Peter's 'plentiful' knees - bare between the top of his long grey socks and bottom of his short grey trousers. He was still busily sucking a sweet that seemed to last forever, he stared at Janine - but said nothing.   "Give us a sweet." Michael begged.

"Can't," Peter replied, "my last one!"   We lazed against the thick foliage of the branches in the warmth of the sun. The sea looked invitingly close from where we were perched. On sunny Sundays such as this, after church, mother would usually take my sister and me to the beach directly below the square, but not today - today everything was different.   Up to now no one else had joined us in the gardens, not even Timmy, the oldest of our group, or Yvonne, Janines younger sister.

"You won't half catch it if your father sees you've climbed that far up again!" Janine warned me.   My father often came and sat in the gardens, - and when he did I made sure not to venture too high!

"You've only got to slip once," he had told me, " and if you do, and fall from that high - should you be lucky enough to still be alive, then you'll probably only have one leg left like me!"

Peter, who had at last finished his sweet, said, "the ice cream man will be here soon."

"It's too early yet." Janine said, but we all checked our pockets to make sure we still had a penny there each. The 'stop me and buy one' man on his tricycle with the tub in front, always came past the gardens at about that time in the mornings and we usually bought one of his penny water ices each. We remained quiet for a while, secretly watching the people going by or standing in small groups talking on the pavements.   Being such a warm morning, many windows were open around the square and we could hear the sounds coming from many different wirelesses.   Before long though, the pavements became deserted and there was a sort of quiet, except for someone talking on the wireless; then, after a short while, everything seemed to happen at once - the wailing of the air raid siren, windows and doors closing, and our mothers rushing into the gardens from various gates and hurrying us into our homes and hopeful safety from an imminent air raid. My mother, Jill and I, quickly descended the back stairs to the unoccupied part of the basement, soon followed by my father and various other residents of the flats at no. 13, with the exception of my grandparents, who grimly refused to budge from their verandah flat.   The musty smell of the basement was something that in nearly another years time we would get used to, but on that day it was a bit overpowering. The general panic quickly subsided as the all clear went, and relief and anticlimax left us all a little bemused.

We soon made our way back up to our ground floor flat. A little later my mother returned me to the gardens and the company of my friends, now including Timmy, who, being a year older than me, and the best climber, immediately ascended to the top of 'our tree,' taking my previous position.   "Where've you been all morning?" I asked him.

"Playing in the catacombs and then sheltering there from the air raid - that is, all except gran and Peter who thought we were silly and refused to come down." Timmy said.   The 'catacombs' were what we called a series of corridors, which lay beneath and beyond the back of no. 36; we often played in these 'eerie' surroundings, which stimulated our imaginations for the games we played.   Peter - not 'our Peter' - was Tims half brother; Monha, his much married mother, had once been married to a 'DeHavilland', from the famous aircraft family, and Peter DeHavilland was about ten years older than Timmy and something of a 'hero' figure to us.   Timmy climbed a little higher, just about reaching the absolute top of the tree.   "I'm looking to see if I can see any German battleships or submarine periscopes" he said - shading his eyes with one hand and holding firmly onto a branch with the other. "Peter said that I was to come and tell him if I saw any." Timmy said importantly.   I looked out to sea and couldn't see anything at all - not even a sail in the distance or a rowing boat closer in shore, usually familiar sights to us from the top of the

13

tree.   Janine and Michael had both sheltered in the basement of Sussex Mansions where their parents had flats on different floors.

"My step father's a first lieutenant now" Michael said, -- "I wonder where he is now?" I waited for Peter, who's father was a flight lieutenant in the Royal Air Force, to say something, but he remained quiet and a little later, as we sat in the tree watching small groups of people having serious discussions on the pavements, he surprised us all by handing round a sweet each.
Janine sucked her sweet quietly, she seemed subdued, she was usually a chatter box.   We were soon all called in for our meals and arranged to meet afterwards - "as long as there are no more air raids" Janine said seriously.

The autumn and early winter of 1939 was a time, when it was, 'things as usual,' but we were aware that anything might happen at any time.   We were more of an audience than participants in the rehearsals for the ugly theatre of war that was soon to be an every day part of our lives, and so we watched and played and did as we were told without too much protest, whilst our parents prepared for the worst and waited for whatever might be thrown at us.   We were soon to get used to many types of rationing, the blackout, carrying gas masks practically every where we went, no go areas, and many other deprivations - but we were also constantly being told of so many, so much worse off than us.

Before the winter really closed in we had formed a routine of play times in the gardens, mostly favouring the larger areas of lawns and country like patches of shrubs, bushes and trees in the bottom gardens.   Although we weren't supposed to, there were good trees to climb here, and many places to hide, and we knew that should there be an air raid, someone would quickly be there to lead us to shelter.

My grandparents decided to move temporarily away from Brighton, to a 'safer' part of the country, and hopefully, far from the probable front line in the event of an invasion.   Albert Redhead, my grandfather, an ex Royal Navy man, and later -

Lincolnshire farmer, was the son of a well known 'one time' mayor of Peterborough, and had once sailed single handedly round the British Isles. He had married his childhood sweetheart Agnes, and after many happy years bringing up their four children, they had decided to settle in Brighton after retiring from the farming world.

After they moved up north to Penrith, number 13 was left in my parents charge. This particularly pleased me because the verandah flat lounge, which was quite large, had a full sized snooker table in it, and my sister and I were allowed to play on this - 'supposedly' under supervision, but when I became reasonably good at the game for my age, I spent quite a bit of time on my own practicing, being very careful "not to rip the cloth", and also remembering the strict instructions from my grandfather, "Never to play on the Sabbath!"

My parents now had to live on my fathers army disability pension and a diminishing bank balance, but none the less, with a little help from a 'philanthropist' relative, it was decided to send me to Brighton College junior school at the beginning of 1941, and up until then I would carry on attending St.Marys Hall kindergarten where my sister Jill, four years older than me, was attending the girls school. My only memories of that kindergarten are sitting on the grass in pleasant warm weather, drinking milk, eating digestive biscuits, and either being read stories, or colouring in pictures.

My friends and I found that being equipped with gas masks was at times something we could turn into a bit of fun, and although at first we had to take them with us everywhere we went, this 'order' often lapsed when we only went as far as the gardens; we always took them with us to school, and also on most other journeys. With food becoming scarcer all the time, as young as we were, we were soon to become acutely aware of the rationing, especially of sweets of course. The thing that affected us most however, was the eventual closure of all the beaches. We were told that, some - or all of them - were being mined, as one of many precautions taken against possible invasion. We could still use the lower slopes for a short time longer, and we still had the use of the bottom gardens down to the tunnel for a while as yet.   Also, we could still use the tunnel, which was now bricked off at the bottom end, as an air raid shelter, if needed.

The closing months of 1939 changed from warm and pleasant, to very wet, and by December, much colder, with regular hard frosts.   The New Year came in with, for us, the war still only something on the radio, but it was still the main topic of conversation for our parents.   The weather in January 1940 also became a focal point of conversation because of its severity, and just for a while the war took second place to the ice and snow and bitterly cold temperatures.   In this kind of weather, my father's type of false leg was something of a drawback, and when icy weather prevailed, anything like a slippery surface was dangerous to him, even with a walking stick, and his balance wasn't helped by another wound to one arm - putting it virtually out of action.

With these handicaps, whenever there was ice and snow about, he became a virtual 'prisoner' indoors. The winter of 1940 was to be no friend to him at all,   with all the ice and eventual heavy falls of snow.   It all started with a rain storm which turned to ice the moment it hit the ground - or indeed wherever it landed;   it was quite spectacular, and we awoke one morning to find the pavements and roads a sheer sheet of ice; the trees in the gardens were also encased in ice, as if crystallised, and blades of grass stood up like tiny icicles in reverse; the whole sight was quite amazing,   everyone agreed that they had never seen anything like it before, and my father resigned him self to more time indoors.

This 'Ice storm' was quickly followed by the first heavy snow falls and record low temperatures.   There were reports of the sea freezing over in places and people skiing on the downs.   In the gardens the snow lay too deeply for properly using Michael's and Peter's home built sledges. Snow-men of varying sizes soon started to appear, and the sea looked greyer and more forbidding than we had ever seen it. We found all types of new and enjoyable activities in the snow, but on the minus side, was the sad sight of a dead bird every here and there. Some of the nearby residents were quick to try and help these freezing birds, who were finding it difficult to get food in the harsh conditions, and scatterings of bread could be seen all over the place, most of these however, quickly became lost to sight with the frequent fresh falls of snow.

"What's that moving over there?" Peter said.

"I think it's a bird" said Janine and immediately started running towards it. We all followed, and there lying on the ground was a bird - still alive - the like of which we had never actually seen in the flesh before.

"It's an owl" Michael said - Janine went to pick it up.

"Careful it doesn't bite you" Peter said.

"What are you going to do with it" I asked Janine.

"Take him home of course", she said "and quickly!"

I felt a twinge of jealousy - I wanted to take it home too! "How do you know it's a him not a her?" I asked her.

"I don't, 'silly' - it's just the way I said it." She looked puzzled as she said this. The round, flat ghost like face of the owl held us in some awe of it; it weakly tried to get out of Janine's hesitant hold, but the effort was short lived and it calmed and just stared from one to another of us with what can only be described as a startled, beseeching look. Janine had been entrusted by her mother with a key to the gardens, "In case of emergencies", she had told her. This to Janine - indeed to all of us - was an emergency. We rushed to the top gate of the gardens and let ourselves out onto the road and soon arrived at Sussex Mansions and took the lift up to her flat on the third floor. Janines' mother, Rosa Sammons, a good friend of my parents, received us with a whole chorus of "oohs" and "aahs" - and told us that the bird was a barn owl, and how it came to be in the gardens was a mystery to her. She relieved Janine of the stricken bird and placed it in a shallow box on a rug near the fire. She tried, at first unsuccessfully, offering it tit bits to eat and warm water to drink. This beautiful owl was kept in their flat for two days, during which time it made a bit of a recovery; then it was taken to a friend's house at Roedean Crescent, where they had the advantage of a fairly large garden, and also lived closer to the sort of environment the bird was likely to have come from. We were very pleased to eventually learn that it was successfully released from there - fully recovered, and when the weather had lost its Arctic bite.

When the snows did finally melt and the harsh winter gave way to the milder weather of early spring, the topic of adult conversations reverted back to the war, and the news from the continent became grimmer by the day, with broadcasts consistently telling of German advances and British retreats. We had already been told of many of the places that would soon be prohibited to us, and one of these was Black Rock open air Bathing pool on the seafront, just below Arundel Terrace. On a dull windy day at the beginning of March 1940, my mother took my sister and me for a last look around this pool, at which we had spent so many enjoyable hours. Although we had mainly used the beaches to swim from, this place had been ideal to use when the sea was rough, and for me in my first years, the paddling pool was also ideal. Now, all the machinery was being stripped out, apparently for war use; it was a depressing scene for the handful of people, and us, who witnessed this, so, somewhat sadly, we walked back along the top of the slopes, past the alcoves, and stopped for a while to watch a shoal of porpoises, dipping and diving, not much more than 200 yards from the shore. In those days these aquatic mammals could be seen from time to time from these beaches. When we arrived home we were introduced to a family who were in the process of moving into the top flat at number 13 - which had been vacated a couple of weeks beforehand by the people who had taken it over from us. Julian, the son of the family, was about my age and we soon became friends.

We were building a new 'secret' camp in the bottom gardens - our last one having been discovered by Ham and Fryer the gardeners, and quickly dismantled by them.   We were all talking about anything in general, but I was bursting to tell them something, and eventually, after Peter had finished laughing at one of his own jokes, I seized my chance.   "Do your parents listen to the 9 o'clock news in the evenings." I asked them.   "Yes of course they do!" Janine quickly replied for all of them.   "Well you know that they give their names before they start reading it," I said, - "well have you ever heard of one of them called Bruce Belfrage?" "Of course we have!"   Janine replied quickly again, but refrained from saying anything else - she looked at the others who all agreed that - " yes they had heard of him."

"Well, since yesterday, he's been living in our house."   I said, 'matter of factly.'

"Has he really?" Peter said.

"Yes, and his son Julian will soon be coming out to play with us- that is after they have got it arranged where he's going to go to school, mother says he'll probably come to St.Mary's Hall with Janine and me in the kindergarten."   From here on in, even we children listened out for the news quite keenly - hoping of course that Bruce Belfrage would be reading it.

During that April, the news from the continent worsened by the day, but on May 11th. when it was announced that a new national government had been formed, with Winston Churchill at the helm, the general feeling was one of relief, and as my father 'echoed' what many people were saying - "at last we've got the right man in the top job!"

The news of the invasions of Holland, Luxemburg, Belgium and France, now of course made the threat of the home shores being invaded even more real, and our parents had some difficulty in hiding their fears from Jill and me. Everything started to take on an air of greater urgency, and the place that was now on everyone's lips was a port on the northern coast of France called Dunkirk, and everyone's thoughts and prayers were now centred on the men of the allied expeditionary force, who were so desperately trying to escape from those hellish beaches and get back to England.

A week or so later I was looking out to sea from the top of 'our tree,' keeping an eye out for anything of a suspicious nature on the calm and deserted sea. "Do you believe in miracles?" I called loudly to the others who were all sitting on branches a bit lower down.

"What sort of miracles?" Peter asked.

"- Well - all of them." I replied hesitantly.

"I do." Janine said.

"So do I", Michael joined in - "why?"

"Because my father says that one has just happened at Dunkirk." I replied. "He says that lots of small boats have rescued hundreds of thousands of soldiers from the beaches there, and brought them safely back to England! He says that some of the boats were from Brighton - you know, the fishing boats and the ones you can go on pleasure trips on, from the beaches."

"What those little rowing boats?" Janine asked in surprise.

"No not them, daft girl," I replied, "the bigger ones with engines in them!"

"I've been on one of those" Peter said. "The summer before last I asked my mother to take me on one, and she did! - she was sick!" he grinned at us, - "so was I." He added, we all laughed.

"You see that house where those men are?" Janine said, we looked at the activity going on, with men coming and going with pieces of furniture into number 25 at the top of the square. - "Well, in a few days time," Janine continued, "that's going to be what they call a workhouse."

"What's a workhouse?" Peter asked.

I answered before Janine could - "My father said it's a place where old men with no money and no homes go to. He told Jill and me that they would be there for as long as the war las   and that we should be polite to them if they spoke to us."

"Why've they come here?" Peter asked.

20

"Because the place that they are at now, at Brighton General Hospital, on the Race Hill, is needed as extra hospital space - at least I think that's it." I said.

At that moment, my mother carrying our old Brownie box camera, came into the gardens and made her way over to our tree.

I remembered that she had told me that morning that I had to tell the others to stay as presentable as possible as she wanted to take a group photograph of us.

"Come on you lot," she said - "down here - I'm going to take a photo of you all together!" She had explained to my father that morning that she still had a couple of shots left to take on the film in the camera, and that she had better take them before there might be any restrictions put on photography and developing and printing. "I'd hoped all of your gang would be here." she said.

But we hadn't seen Tim or Julian all that day - there were just the four of us.

"Come on, - Michael - you on the left - Peter - you next to Michael- Janine, you next, and then you David." She soon had us organised, and we dutifully lined up for a photograph which we would never see, due to something happening at the chemist where it was taken to be printed. A pity, it would have made a good picture, with Michael, tall for his age and slim, fair and serious - Peter, a bit shorter - plumpish, and dark haired, and Janine, just slightly plumpish, with freckles and a mop of brown curly hair - and lastly me, with the same build as Michael, but with a shock of what everyone called - 'bright red' hair. I always remember overhearing a comment about my hair from one lady to another sitting on one of the gardens seats. "It's not fair is it," she said, "such a beautiful head of hair on such a horrible little boy!"

We were well aware that we were not too popular with some of the people who used the gardens. We climbed trees and shouldn't have done, we often walked over 'sacred' flower beds to retrieve a ball or to look in some bush to see if there were any birds nests there; we were permanently hiding from the gardeners, and although we were taught to be polite, we were none the less, noisy and somewhat self centred - in other words just children being children.

With the possibility of invasion becoming increasingly more likely, even more people moved away from the square, but before long these movements were restricted because the authorities were determined to prevent a mass panic which would obviously lead to a chaotic exodus.

Eventually a large heavy naval gun was installed at the top of Dukes Mound on the seafront below Lewes Crescent - also an observation tower for this gun was built on the lawn of the south west corner of the bottom gardens. The loud explosions from this gun being used in practice, shook the ground we stood on and cracked some of the windows of the houses nearby that hadn't been secured with tape or reinforced in some way. After each explosion - if the winds were coming from a southerly direction - clouds of yellow smoke would drift up the crescent, leaving an acrid taste in your mouth if you happened to be caught unawares and inhaled the pungent fumes.

It now became inevitable that many more restrictions on our movements were soon to come, and although we did our best to carry on with every day life as normally as possible, there was a tension in the air that even we children were aware of. Sublimely perhaps, everyone carried on in the hope that around the next corner there might be a little better news. This though was not to be, and around that 'corner' the skies would soon be the hunting areas of hostile aircraft, hell bent on destroying us, and it was going to be a long time before we could take for granted that any day would be a peaceful one!

CHAPTER TWO.

Some elderly visitors. -- Threat of invasion. – A dilemma
for the schools. – The Odeon - a direct hit!

The 'old men' quickly became established in the house at the top of the square, which had been newly adapted as their home.   They were mainly a bunch of cheerful characters; most of them clothed identically in herring bone jackets and grey trousers or trousers to match. They all wore black shoes or boots and quite a few of them wore caps; all this adding up to an unmistakable identity. "Why don't they give them all uniforms and be done with it?!"   My father expressed his anger for these unfortunate fellow human beings, whom officialdom, he thought, had robbed of individual identity.   In a way though, he was wrong there - because amongst them were many real characters, that we would eventually get to know quite well.   Most of them we liked, some we never got to know, and just a few, we loathed!

In the main they got on quite well with most of us who lived in the square; but a few of the residents made no effort at all to hide their disgust of them! The only thing that did warrant disgust from all of us, was the continual spitting - which left spatters of phlegm here and there around the roads of the square - they usually, at least, kept this off the pavements!   A rumour went around that they had been encouraged to spit by whoever dealt with their medical side; "something to do with preventing tuberculosis," someone told my father - but just a rumour; however the general feeling was - "they are here for the war so lets make the best of it and try to live together in harmony."   A small group of ladies did have a go at trying to get a petition signed to have the men removed.   Under the circumstances, this was mainly met with the contempt it deserved, in particular by my father, who expressed himself to these ladies in no uncertain terms, giving them very short shrift indeed; from there on in he was completely ignored by them.   "Something," he told us, "which doesn't lose me any sleep at all!"   As time went by these men became a part of the community and during the years to come, contributed to many incidents which brightened our lives in those difficult times.

With many of the schools now posed with the problem of, should they stay where they were, or should they evacuate if possible to some 'safer' part of the country; St.Marys Hall, in particular, was uncertain as to it's immediate future. My sister's and my own schooling was something very much on our parents minds, indeed, wherever schools were that could be in the front line if an invasion came - the parents there were all faced with the same dilemma.
     My father had a cousin with a small farm in Surrey, and it had been arranged that, if the worst came to the worst, we could go there for a while; however the move was something they wanted to avoid if possible, especially having to go through all the rigmarole of arranging for us to go to schools in that area.   My parents were determined to try to stay in Brighton and avoid all the upheaval, so they decided to wait and see what the schools came up with.   We soon found out that some schools had decided to evacuate. Roedean school for girls would go to Keswick in the north. Brighton College decided to stay where it was, and the preparatory school, renamed 'junior school', under the headmastership of Mr.F.L.B.Stokes, with just 37 boys remaining, transfered from Lewes Crecent to Bristol House in the main college on the Eastern Road.   Mr.Grassen had taken another 60 boys with him to Birkhampstead. St.Marys Hall, the oldest school in Brighton, was still undecided, and this of course affected both my sister and myself.   It had been hoped that I would stay at the kindergarten

until the end of 1940. On the 19th of May 1940 a letter from the head mistress, Miss.E.Stopford, to parents, had said that they believed, after reassurances from the A.R.P. (air raid precaution) authorities, that the school could carry on as it was; after all it had been pointed out that the evacuation would be rather futile as the west country and the north would be just as exposed to attack as the south east! However a little later another letter from Miss.Stopford explained to parents that because, mainly for financial reasons, the school couldn't afford to evacuate, she asked parents to let her know by no later than Thursday morning, June 25th, whether they were unwilling to send their daughters back to St.Marys Hall - or were doubtful - or wished their daughters to go to some other school. Finally a letter from Mr.A.C.Elliot, the school chairman, dated 28th June 1940 confirmed that the response of the majority of parents was to have their daughters sent to other schools and therefore St.Marys Hall would close forthwith for the duration of the war. Soon after our parents received this letter, it was decided that my sister would go to Brighton and Hove High School for girls, and that I would have private tuition until joining Brighton College Junior School at the beginning of the summer term 1941.

With all the beaches now no go areas, we found ourselves missing our frequent summer swims very much, particularly mother, who now took to taking my sister and me - sometimes with friends - for walks on the nearby downs. We would leave the square and walk past the 'Orange Hue' cafe and bakery, where on Saturdays we always bought a special cake for the weekends, then carry on over the highest point of that part of the downs, just past the golf club, and then going - somewhat dangerously - between a tee and a green, which the path ran through the middle of; we would descend into Ovingdean and past the famous 'Ovingdean Grange'. This was the same big house written of in the book of that name by William Harrison Ainsworth. The book, which is mainly fictional, tells of the 'flight' of Charles II from Cromwell's armies, and how he hid there for a time. This large, beautiful old house, covered in Virginia Creeper at that time, always conjured up visions of ghostly happenings in my already imaginative mind; in later years it would seem even more eerie, when walking past there in the twilight of summer evenings and seeing bats darting here and there above the chimney pots in the fading light, and perhaps also occasionally hearing the haunting call of an owl, thus giving the grange, the nearby church and the farm buildings, an intriguing and mystical aura in my mind.   My mother particularly liked to visit St.Wulfran's, the beautiful Norman built church here; probably, architecturally, one of the best of its kind seen over the traverse of the downs.   In a letter to me from Mr.J.G.Davies - Ovingdean historian, Mr.Davies quotes from his work, 'A Historical Gazateer of Ovingdean Ecclesiastical Parish':-

"A little church at Ovingdean is mentioned in the Domesday Book (1086) - the nave and chancel of today's St.Wulfran's are probably 1066 - 1086, or a little later - the tower is probably 1216 and contains a 1430 bell."

Between Ovingdean and Woodingdean, and also within easy walking distance, especially for youthful limbs, was a spinney consisting of briar,a few small trees, and many kinds of shrubbery.

In late August and September parties of us would collect large amounts of blackberries from here, often finding the empty nests of many varieties of birds that found the thick cover an ideal place to rear their young.   Rabbits abounded here, and it was also evident that foxes found this a happy hunting ground.

Towards the end of July 1940, on a beautiful hot summer's day, we picnicked by a corn field on a high part of the downs - halfway on our regular walk.   Below us and about a quarter of a mile away, on the other side of a small valley which was now lush with green corn, was Roedean School, and beyond that the calm blue sea stretching to a hazy horizon; there wasn't a boat to be seen, just the seagulls circling and gliding near the edge of the cliffs, completed this idyllic scene. Apart from an occasional aeroplane heading towards France, the sky, in all it's peaceful blue, was the thoroughfare for the larks and their unforgettable singing as they soared and hovered above us. Breathing in this air of high summer downland, tainted by refreshing salt breezes, was, as my mother poetically put it, "a luxury surely designed by the gods to make the soul wish, at least to linger - perhaps to stay." All too soon we started the journey back home, and when nearly there, our calmed nerves were quickly shattered by the ominous sound of the air raid siren. Jill and I quickly joining our mother, grabbed a hand each and half walked and half ran to the safety of indoors - now less than half a mile away. My father was waiting on the doorstep for us and we quickly descended to the basement and the part of it that had been chosen the best place to be - should a bomb fall on the house! This area had been temporarily furnished as comfortably as possible for whenever we might have to shelter there. There were a couple of old armchairs, that had certainly seen better days, some deck chairs that would normally have been used on the beach or in the gardens, a couple of small tables and a sort of a sideboard which some previous tenant had left behind and which now contained some soft drinks for when necessary, and some stronger drinks which my parents owned up to calling - 'Dutch courage!'

One particular idea of my mother's was that Jill and I should have a hammock each to sleep in if necessary; these had been precariously hung across the basement hall, just beside all the seats. We did eventually use these hammocks at nights in the height of the bombings, but they were also a great source of amusement to us and our friends at other times. We stayed in the basement for about twenty minutes and then the all clear went. We had heard no actual air raid at all and before long I was allowed into the top gardens to play until teatime.

"You see that man sitting over there with my uncle Keith." said Janine. Michael and I looked over at the pale faced man in army uniform sitting with Janines uncle on a seat at the other end of the gardens. Janine continued, "He's just come out of hospital - he's one of the soldiers to escape from Dunkirk!" We looked at him with greater interest. "He's Brenda Bassett's uncle," Janine said, "he's staying with them for a few days." Brenda had occasionally played with us in the gardens when we had felt like inviting her. We knew better than to go over and listen to them without an invitation, none the less, we were tempted - getting away from Dunkirk sounded very thrilling to us and I hoped to find out more later of his adventure from Janine, after she had spoken to her uncle.

"That stripe on his arm means he's a Lance Corporal." Janine said.

"Is he going to do any more fighting?" Michael asked.

"Yes - I suppose so - when he's better!" Janine answered. We looked at him again, a bit more closely this time, and couldn't see anything wrong with him.

"He must have wounds you can't see!" said Michael.

"Yes, it's something like that." Janine said, but once again looked puzzled as she said it.

"My dad says we're going to need every man we can get if there's going to be an invasion, he told us that now we've got all those men back from Dunkirk, we'd stand a good fighting chance if it came to that!" I said knowledgeably.

"Well we won't be here if that comes," Janine said "we're going to Wales; - my father says there won't be an invasion there! I think Peter and his mother are coming with us too." Peter nodded affirmatively, trying not to open his mouth and show us he was secretly sucking another sweet. I was about to ask Janine to tell us more about this when we heard the gate nearest to number thirteen shutting, and my father, using a necessary walking stick, made his way carefully over to where the soldier and Janine's uncle were sitting. They stayed there, in earnest conversation, until mother called us in for tea. That evening my father told us about Lance Corporal Bassett's escape and eventual rescue at Dunkirk. He had been one of the last soldiers of the British expeditionary force who had avoided being captured by the Germans as they had advanced on the beaches. He had suffered shell shock and a wounded shoulder, but was now recovering quite well.   My parents carried on talking long after my sister and I had gone to bed. I lay awake for quite some time - in some ways it all seemed rather exciting to me - but innocent as I was at that age, I sensed very clearly the intense air of apprehension.

The news that the Channel Islands had been taken by the Germans affected Michaels mother, Bunty, a special friend of my mothers, very badly - she had close relatives who lived on Guernsey, and not knowing exactly what was going on there, was extremely worrying - not only for her, but also a neighbour of ours who's mother also lived on Guernsey.

Before long the air raids increased in intensity and we quite often found ourselves the spectators to amazing aerial battles that suddenly materialized - literally from out of the blue.   The German onslaught on this country now became devastating and the battle for Britain had begun in earnest.   Fierce aerial 'dog fights' appeared and disappeared with frightening speed, and the aircraft taking part left wispy trails of white vapour behind them in the clear blue skies.   The job of sounding the siren for all these 'deadly duels' was practically an impossibility, and we often found ourselves in the gardens whilst they suddenly took place without any warning.   At these times we usually sought what protection we could, in case the enemy should decide to machine gun us, behind the thickest and largest of the trees.   On one occasion a German fighter suddenly flew very low over the gardens, shaking us considerably; however we felt a bit better when this enemy aircraft was quickly followed by a spitfire, hot in pursuit and loudly cheered by a small group of people on the nearby pavement.

"Did you see the pilot in that spitfire, David," Tim called over to me from where he stood behind the inadequate cover of a small bush.   Still shaking slightly, I replied "Yes". - But I wasn't sure really; I had noticed the cockpit, but it had all happened so quickly that what was inside it had only been a blur.   This incident, which was over in only a few seconds, has engraved itself on my mind, and, to this day, I still wonder how these antagonists - going at such enormous speeds - had missed crashing into the tall houses of Sussex Square.

Our visits to the comparative safety of the basement now became a bit more frequent. In August and September bombs badly damaged several streets in Brighton, some near to us, but the square and crescents and gardens were unscathed.

One day early in September, a few of us, including my sister and a few of her friends had been playing rounders on the lawn in the top gardens, and feeling somewhat hot had decided to have half time. We lazed on the grass near to the seat my father was sitting on - reading the previous night's copy of The Evening Argus. My mother and Rosa Sammons came into the gardens, each carrying a large jug of ice cold squash and some cups; - everyone was given a cup full. My father who thought it was a good thing to try to keep everyone's morale up during these distressing times, chose this moment to read a piece from the paper to us all - calling for our attention he read:-

"A Hurricane pilot forced down an ME 109 during Saturday's battle over Kent, after he had used up his ammunition in shooting down two enemy fighters. I saw a third ME109 dive past me. I followed him down to ground level and chased him southwards," he said "he did not rise above a hundred feet until well south of Maidstone then he throttled back. I overtook him and flew alongside him, pointing downwards to the ground. He turned away, so I carried out a dummy quarter attack, breaking away very close to him. After this he landed his ME109 in a field at about 140 miles per hour. I saw the pilot get out, apparently unhurt, and as I circled round him he put his hands above his head, so I waved to him and he waved back. Then I circled low over him and threw him a packet of twenty cigarettes which I had with me. I saw him pick them up, and again he waved. Then I saw what I believed to be members of the Home Guard go into the field and take him prisoner. After that I returned to my base."'

For quite some time it had been a fairly regular custom of my mother's, on Saturday afternoons, to take my sister and me to the Odeon cinema in Kemptown - that is, if the film was deemed to be suitable and if nothing else had been planned - we eagerly looked forward to these outings. The little Odeon, as we called it because there was another larger Odeon cinema in Brighton, showed three programmes a week. One from Monday to Wednesday, then one from Thursday to Saturday, and on Sunday a couple of older films, made up a good varied week of cinema going. There were usually two films per programme, with the news and trailers showing in between them. We always sat upstairs in the two and threepennies; the stalls were cheaper, and if two U certificate films were showing - in other words films when children under sixteen years of age could go in unaccompanied by an adult - the front stalls would normally be packed out by a very young audience, who were quick to cheer the heroes and even quicker to jeer at the bad guys. The usherettes and the manager had their work cut out to stop kids jumping all over the seats and non payers stealthily creeping in through the emergency exits. Quite often, during the 'boring bits'- paper missiles or heavier objects could be seen in flight above the heads of the audience; however, it was the pictures that everyone had come to see, and for most of the time one could watch in relative peace.

On Saturday September 14th. 1940, my mother told my sister and me that there would be no pictures that day because she was going to visit a friend who had just been discharged from hospital after an operation, to convalesce at home. She said that she didn't want us to go on our own, even if she could make sure that we got in alright - her friend lived in a street not far from the cinema. We were disappointed, but there would be other Saturdays.

That afternoon, Janine and I were the only ones in the top gardens. "Lets see if there are any mulberries left." Janine suggested. We usually picked these in July and August, but

31

sometimes you could still find the odd one or two right into September.   We ambled over to the north easterly corner of the gardens where the mulberry tree was, to see what fruit there was in the middle of it.   "There's one or two in that corner over there," I pointed to where there were several branches with just a few berries on them;   I was about to tell Janine that I would go first - when the explosion came; a huge terrifying noise! -- Janine screamed, and immediately started running for the gate on her side of the square, she had her emergency key with her.   I ran for the opposite gate, which I knew I could quickly climb over, but by the time I got there Mrs.Belfrage had opened it for me; my father was waiting anxiously on the doorstep.   We quickly went indoors and downstairs to the basement, where Julian and two of the other residents were already taking shelter.   After a while everything went quiet and my father left me with Mrs.Belfrage and the others and returned upstairs to our flat - "to make a phone call," he said. It had sounded as if the bombs had gone off somewhere in the direction of the part of Kemptown that my mother had gone to that afternoon.   A little later I returned to our flat - everything seemed quiet now - I can't remember anything at all about sirens or all clears.   I found my father with my sister, who had just returned from a friends house in the square, trying to find out - if they could - anything about where and what had been hit, and in particular about the huge first explosion. He rang several people to find out if they had seen my mother - the friend that she was visiting wasn't on the phone - however, all this was to no avail.   Jill was near to tears, my father red faced and very anxious, and I had begun to fret; but, just as I was about to burst into tears, the phone went and the sudden relieved look on my fathers face spoke for itself.   I managed to suppress any outbursts as my father told us that mother was alright, and that she would be home in about an hour or so. In a little over an hour, she arrived home, somewhat dishevelled, but otherwise all in one piece. She had been helping a couple of boys, who had slight injuries, up to the hospital.   Immediately after the bombing she had left off from her friends flat to get home as quickly as possible, but, on being told by a passer by that the Odeon had been hit, she decided to head in that direction and see if there was anything she could do; there were other people hurrying to get there as well. When she arrived there she found that the cinema had received a direct hit. To her horror, she saw that bodies were laid out on the ground just outside it - these, heartbreakingly, included some dead children. There were many people there helping, including doctors, nurses, ambulance men, air raid wardens and members of the general public, - and what had been chaotic pandemonium, was now, slowly, coming under efficient control. An air raid warden asked my mother and another lady to escort one child, bleeding from high up on his leg, but still able to walk, and another slightly older boy, with cuts - who although dazed - was also still able to walk, to the Sussex County Hospital no more than 100 yards away. They arrived there to find this place also coming grimly and efficiently under control, and there seemed to be injured and shocked people everywhere.

It was from the hospital that she had managed to get to a phone to let us know she was alright. After delivering the two boys to the hospital she had returned to the scene of devastation at the Odeon - helping where she could, and all the time fiercely trying not to break down and cry for the dead and wounded, at the same time as offering countless prayers of thanks that we hadn't gone to the cinema that afternoon. An hour later, on leaving this scene of devastation, where rescue work was still going on - and would do for quite some time - she had then walked back home in something of a daze, hardly believing all that had happened in the course of nearly two hours of nightmare! She arrived home to one very grateful family, now all fussing around her. She sipped from a strong and soothing drink, and then the tears came - readily and deeply!

That Saturday was one of the darkest days of the war in Brighton, - with 55 people killed in the cinema and various streets that had also been hit by a string of bombs that had fallen in a westerly line from the Odeon cinema to Rock Gardens.   There was, apart from the stories of the exemplary behaviour of all who were there to help, one particularly uplifting story that quickly spread around.   Three small boys, with a small amount of change in their pockets, were on their way to the cinema that afternoon, and on the way there they had spent some of this money on sweets and things; then they found, when they got there, that they hadn't got enough money for their admittances - so they turned around and went back home.   If they had got in, they would have been sitting somewhere in the front stalls - which was the part of the cinema where the worst of the casualties were!

After this horrific raid, the enemy, had in our view, become much worse than just 'the enemy'; the cold fury that everyone now felt towards them was summed up in the Evening Argus edition of Monday 16th September 1940, --- "they were", the Argus said "Evil Monsters!"

Early that evening I accompanied my parents for a walk around the bottom gardens; whilst they stood talking to some people at the top of the slope near the tunnel, a part of the gardens that would soon have barbed wire stretched 'concertina style' across it, a German aeroplane, only a small distance away and heading out to sea, jettisoned it's bomb load into the sea - somewhere close to the shore.   We hurried to the shelter of the tunnel, but there were no explosions and no sirens.   We soon walked home, my mother and father in deep conversation, and me, alert, a little frightened, and glad to be close to them.

On the Wednesday evening of the next week the sirens went off at about the same time as I was getting ready to go to bed, so once again we all trooped down to the basement. Quite soon after arriving there we heard some explosions, but although they were quite loud, we none the less knew that they must have come from half a mile or so away.   A bit later, when the all clear had gone, we returned upstairs - there was no further enemy activity that night.   The next morning we heard that White Street, near Edward Street, not very far from us, had been hit - killing eleven people; this number included a family of five!   This news saddened us all of course; but in particular my mother, who reminded us that a cleaning lady who had worked for my grandparents before the war, lived in White Street.   A bit later that day she went to find out about her - fortunately this lady was quite alright, but the street had suffered very severe damage, with some of the houses completely demolished, and of course many of the people who lived there and nearby, were deeply shocked.   It was yet another terrible air raid - and all within five days!   Just two days after this, whilst using the shelter once again, we heard what was obviously another bad raid; this time it was the Lewes Road area that had been hit, with more loss of life.

My mother had arranged to take a party of us blackberrying on Sunday September 22nd., we would usually have gone earlier than this, but of course the present circumstances prevented us doing so, however this particular date had been set before all these horrific raids, so she took the time to go and see the parents of all those who had been invited to go with us and see if they still wanted their children to go.   Without exception they all agreed that the outing should go ahead - unless of course an air raid was taking place at the time; so on that Sunday, my mother -   rather like a female version of the Pied Piper -   took my sister and me with some of my sisters friends, and some of mine, for a walk over the downs to collect blackberries.   Being a little later this year than usual was "better late than never", she reminded us.   There were no aeroplanes at all, just the skylarks soaring up into a cloudless sky.
The golfers were out in force and we all quickly passed the dangerous part where golfballs were likely to come from out of the blue, where the path crossed the fairway - or was it perhaps the other way around!   "It wouldn't do to have missed being hit by the bombs, -- only to be laid flat by a golf ball."   My mother

laughed at her own joke. We politely joined in. The blackberry patch, was a rambling, uneven, two acres of briar entwined and entangled between various small trees and thick bushes of varying heights. These offered good places to play hide and seek to those of us who preferred this to allowing our fingers to get too close to fat little spiders sitting firmly in the centres of immaculately spun webs, that seemed to adorn everywhere where the best fruit hung in inviting clusters. We all picked for a while though, and no pair of hands escaped the scratches or reddish, purplish blue stains from this wild harvest. For lunch we shared sun warmed lemonade, paste sandwiches - over filled with home grown mustard and cress, and there was also some luke warm tea from a couple of ancient flasks. Now and again we caught sight of a rabbit hastily disappearing to somewhere in the underbrush or to one of the many warrens in evidence, seemingly everywhere. No one even glimpsed a fox, but we constantly kept watch on the large holes dug into the steeper parts of the downs near to us. The bird population, obviously at first annoyed with us for our intrusion, soon took little notice of us, but we were always aware of their constant chattering and darting to and fro. Even a kestrel hovered close by - looking down as if we might be its next prey!

"Why are there never any eggs in the nests we keep finding?" asked Peter.

"You only find those in spring time, silly!" - said Janine.

"Why's that?" Peter asked.

Janine hesitated for a moment - then said - "Because that's the time they like to bring their baby birds up."

"Why's that?" Peter stubbornly asked again.

"Oh I don't know", Janine answered impatiently, "mummy says it's got something to do with the birds and the bees!"

"What have the bees got to do with it?" Peter asked.

My mother laughed and said it was time to make tracks for home, and with baskets well laden with blackberries, which would make pies and jams and wines, and keep several mothers busy for a while, we trooped back over the downs - past the golfers again, who, if hacking away at a golf ball stuck under a thick tuft of grass, were careful to show 'good sportsmanship', as we noisily passed by. Eventually - tired, healthy and hungry, we arrived back home.

For the best part of a day the gardens had had peace from us - but tomorrow was another day!

That night I slept without being disturbed and my dreams envisioned nothing more frightening than small spiders resembling shelled hazelnuts, with legs, - all defiantly protecting their finely constructed homes from marauding giants - by sitting in the middle of their webs and giving us the 'evil eye'!

A few days later there was another big raid with many casualties - this time in the Albion Hill area of Brighton. By now though, we were keyed up to expect the worst at any time; yet, in the midst of all the adversity, there was still a stoic sense of humour, and always an enormous feeling of camaraderie, with everyone mucking in together and making the most of it. This attitude, which was adopted by so many during those difficult times, was what helped us to endure the hours of danger, and then carry on with everyday life as normally as possible.

CHAPTER THREE

Dog fights. – The water tank. – Air raids.

The closing months of 1940 seemed to bring an awareness in us all of changing attitudes and ways of life among the many people we knew, or slightly knew, who lived near to us.   Our parents quite often had lengthy conversations with people, who up until then, they had only been on 'nodding' acquaintances with; also the attitudes towards us children playing in the gardens, were now more relaxed and tolerant.   The men from the workhouse were now becoming settled in - many of them were called by their Christian names, but some like 'Kingy' preferred surnames; some of them soon got nicknames, a few of which were none too flattering though!   The one we called Kingy - or Mr.King, if addressing him, used to be a boot black at Brighton station, and smoked a pipe which fascinated everyone who saw it; it was like one would imagine the head of a fierce tribal warrior would look like, with spikes coming out of either side of it - as if they were sharpened bones that had been pierced through the nose and cheeks - you never saw Kingy without this pipe.   Another man, who we called Frank, was unlike the others in more ways than one, he obviously took time to keep the clothes he was supplied with in very good order; he was quiet, well spoken, good mannered and shy.   He intrigued my father in particular, but, try as hard as he did, he couldn't get Frank to disclose anything of his past - that is not until the end of the war and it was time for these men to leave the square.   One man, who was definitely not quite right in the head, but very mild mannered and totally inoffensive, we called 'Dopey' - after one of the seven dwarfs; we had a few laughs at poor old Dopey's expense, but he always joined in and laughed with us - I like to think that we were never cruel.

The air raids persisted - at first mostly in the daytime - but eventually came the night raids.

My bed-time was just before nine o'clock, and it was thought that I would probably be asleep by the time everyone had settled down to listen to the nine o'clock news; more often than not though I was still awake and could hear what was going on from the bedroom I still shared with my sister - the door was always left slightly ajar. It wasn't so much the actual news I tried to hear - that was mostly 'French' to me, but any comments my parents might make about what was being said - I just liked to hear the sounds.

Being woken from a nice warm bed in the middle of the night to go to the shelter of the basement, was one of the things I protested about the most. At the beginning of a night raid, mother would usher my sister and me, both wearing our dressing gowns, down the stairs, soon to be joined by father - and usually some of the other residents. Whatever time it actually was, didn't really matter to me - I just termed it the middle of the night! I can remember on some nights when we were sheltering, Bruce Belfrage would come and join his wife and Julian, and it seemed odd, that just a few hours beforehand, he had been reading out the news to the nation. On those first raids, when not much happened, I quickly got into my hammock - on some nights I would immediately fall asleep again - and the next day hardly remember a thing, not even going back up to bed again when the all clear had gone. On other nights I would stay awake listening to all the conversation whilst amusing myself by trying to make the hammock swing from side to side; at other times though, if the raid was a bad one, and the explosions, loud and seeming to come from close by, I would make it quite clear that I wanted to get out of the hammock and stay as close as possible to my reassuring parents.

These raids were particularly frightening, and despite knowing that we were in the 'safest' part of the house, we none the less felt very vulnerable.   The harsh whistling sounds from the bombs falling close to the square, or seemingly close, were - to say the least - terrifying!   I can remember clamping my hands tightly over my ears and also firmly closing my eyes with each whistle - hopefully muffling the worst of the explosions.   At the end of each of these raids, when the drone of the German bombers could no longer be heard and the explosions had given way to suspenseful silence, we would wait impatiently for the all clear, and when that came - make our way back upstairs to our long deserted beds, and perhaps, uneasy sleep.   Usually, after such a night, the daylight hours would be air raid free, but not always, there were sometimes quick 'hit and run' raids made by 'prowlers' coming in quickly from the sea - dropping their bombs on whoever happened to be unfortunate that day, and maybe even machine gunning the streets, before disappearing out to sea again.

During those winter months, my mother's efforts at giving me some sort of tuition at home in place of school, were somewhat spasmodic, but at that age professional tuition was not imperative - just the effort was good enough.   Although I was well able to read for myself, I was sometimes read to from the better known childrens classics.   I remember, when I was suffering from measles, she was reading to me, in a slightly darkened room, from 'Alice in Wonderland.'

"Do you know," mother said rhetorically "that Lewis Carrol, the man who wrote this, lived two doors away from here at number eleven for a while - his real name was the Reverend Charles Dodgson - but he called himself Lewis Carrol when he was writing books. There is a story ," mother continued, " that whilst he was taking a nap under one of the 'Cypress Macrocarpa'. - "

" -- the what?" I asked.

Mother laughed, "that's the Latin name given to the fir trees in the gardens - I prefer to call them by their American name - Monterey

Cypress; in any case, to continue - whilst he was sleeping under the tree, probably the one that you climb the most, he had a strange dream, and this dream eventually led to him writing what I'm reading to you now - Alice in Wonderland." I thought about this for a while, and have often thought about it since - I like to think that it really did happen like that.

During November and December there were more air raids, and getting up in the middle of the night became a fairly regular occurrence.   When we sheltered from these raids and the bombing could be loudly heard, I always had a horrible wrenching feeling in my stomach, and the faces of those around me couldn't hide the fear in their eyes, and those images of deep anxiety, are still sketched in my mind.   On the quieter nights, when I wasn't sleeping, there were books to read, but it was difficult to concentrate, especially in the poor light.

At the approach of dark every night, the black out was strictly adhered to, and woe betide the house that let even a glimmer of light be seen by a passing air raid warden, who, on seeing it, would shout out loudly, something like - - "PUT THAT BLOODY LIGHT OUT!"   At this loudly audible command, all eyes would quickly glance at the shutters or blinds to make sure they were firmly shut or tightly pulled together.

That winter was a cold one again, with more frost, ice and snow; however, it wasn't as bad as the previous one, when the 'ice storm' had been what everyone termed, " a once in a lifetime happening."   On Christmas eve my sister and some of her friends formed a small group to go carol singing, and begrudgingly - on the insistence of my mother - after I had spent all day pleading with her, I was allowed to go with them. Carol singing in the blackout was quite a novelty, but a bit difficult in the dark; however, we were alright in the houses that had flats and where we could get into the front door, making it possible to sing outside the individual flats.   The hallways leading to these flats usually had push button lights - the ones that light for about thirty seconds, when pushed, and abruptly go out again. We always had it organised that one of us would stand by the switch and keep the singers supplied with light. In previous years we had used homemade lanterns, but now, just a couple of battery torches were shared between us, which, when out in the blackout, we tried to keep 'muffled'. Fortunately we all knew most of the words to the carols and so needed no word sheets or hymn books to sing from. Sometimes some young 'wag' would use his or her own words, usually causing much giggling amongst us, but mostly the carol singing was taken seriously and we sung well, and were thus appreciated. At many of the places we sang at, we were expected and were often asked for an encore - which would mean singing another carol - this, we did gladly. Despite the rationing we were often given sweets, homemade cakes, and sometimes some fruit, as well as the coins, which were also quite generously given.

Some people asked what the money they gave was for, and we always told them, quite honestly, that after it had been equally divided amongst us, we would probably buy presents with it. We never sang for charity, but we were always generous with what we received and consequently some of the men from the workhouse found themselves with small gifts of tobacco, which we would pay our parents to purchase for us, and pockets and purses that had jingled quite heavily whilst the shops were closed over the Christmas period - soon reverted to the familiar sound of emptiness.

On Christmas morning, Jill and I eagerly awoke early to find the customary exciting pillow cases, stuffed with parcels of varying sizes, at the foot of our beds. These parcels, we would try to feel out with our feet in excitng anticipation of what they might turn out to be. After what seemed an eternity, our mother came into our bedroom and turned on the light before kissing us a happy Christmas - thus signalling an immediate start on opening the presents. From the open door of the bedroom we could see through to where the Christmas tree stood; brightly decorated with glass balls of varying colours, strands of tinsel, some tiny parcels in bright wrapping paper, which would be handed out to us and our guests at tea time, and a large star adorning the top.   Attached to many of the branches were small candles, which would also be lit that evening in the darkened room - thereby transforming the familiar surroundings into something more magical for just a short while. During the morning, after a late breakfast, and when all the wrapping paper had been folded and put away, perhaps to be used on another day, the first of the visitors started to appear.   These were friends of my parents who had been invited round for a drink of something - usually a bit stronger than tea or coffee.   A little later my father went to meet some of his friends for a drink at his local, 'The Rock Inn', and mother, preferring to be left alone to get on with cooking the Christmas dinner, gladly allowed my sister and me to go out for a while.   We each went our own ways, and spent the next hour or so visiting friends, perhaps showing off a new present, and remembering to heed the advice or warning not to ruin our appetites for our Christmas meal, by eating too many sweets or mince pies; just for a day or so the rationing was apparently forgotten.   A bit later, back at home, we enjoyed the luxury of a roast chicken with all the trimmings; this was followed by a rich Christmas pudding into which several silver threepenny pieces had been more or less strategically placed.

In the early evening when our guests had arrived, and everyone had a piece of Christmas cake and a drink in their hands, all but one of the lights were put out and the candles on the tree were lit.
Tiny presents were handed down from the tree to us children, and the time left before bedtime flew past in a mist of happy activity.
That night I slept a sleep of contentment, uninterrupted by the nightmare of air raids.

The air raids started again on the twenty seventh of December; almost as though a Christmas lull had been arranged.   On that day, and quite frequently during the weeks to come, we had to take shelter from what often turned out to be, just a solitary raider.

These raiders were usually sent packing by a heavy barrage from the ground artillery, which by this stage of the war, had grown considerably in strength and improved quite spectacularly in accuracy!

During the early months of 1941 there were many air raids. The 'Blitz' continued mainly in London and other strategic targets, but Brighton got quite a mauling as well, and continued getting raids by night and by day, which did quite a bit of structural damage, and of course the casualties continued to spiral.

During the winter of 1941 I witnessed our main play area in the top gardens being transformed by the building of a large static water tank - this tank - when completed, took over the whole of the lawn where we used to play cricket, rounders and football; it was built, of course, for the fire brigade to use in the event of fires caused by the bombing; it was a sunken construction looking very much like a swimming pool, and in the very early days when the water was still clean, some of the more adventurous of us risked taking a quick dip in this 'pool' on the warmer days of early summer, but this was sternly discouraged by our parents and the authorities, and in any case the water soon became too dirty to contemplate doing so any more.

Because of the changes in the top gardens after the installation of the water tank, my parents, when they used these gardens, now placed their deck chairs near to our favourite tree where there was still some grass, and just a few yards away from the water tank.

My father, preferred to read his morning paper indoors at breakfast time, but the reason that he always brought the previous night's copy of the Evening Argus out in the gardens with him, if the weather was suitable, was because after he had quickly scanned through it when it arrived, he allowed my mother and anyone else who wanted to read it, to keep it for the rest of the evening. On a pleasant winters day towards the latter half of February he read out from the previous nights paper the following.

Headed,

'YOU ARE FUNNY PEOPLE'. - The small article read.

Colonel G.Symonds, inventor of the stirrup pump, said in London today, that at first they had difficulty in finding the right kind of nozzle for it.

"We had heard of the Bordeaux nozzle - which is used for spraying the vine," he said, "so we wrote to Paris but they had never heard of it. - Then we wrote to Bordeaux."

"You are funny people," they replied, "we get our nozzles from Birmingham!"

Also printed in thats night's Argus - which he read out to a friend of his sitting nearby, were the following grim statistics:

During January in Great Britain,

KILLED

MEN -- 720
WOMEN -- 567
CHILDREN UNDER 16 -- 189

INJURED

MEN -- 1172
WOMEN -- 682
CHILDREN UNDER 16 -- 158

The newspapers and the radio kept us well informed of what was happening in other parts of the country, and even when we were having a comparatively quiet period, we were none the less aware of other peoples suffering.

"Giving us these statistics" my father said, "essentially gives us the true picture, and I firmly believe that we need to be told - if there had been any cover up of the more grim facts it would have deprived us of that feeling of everyone being in the same boat, and everyone pulling together to end the nightmare and return to peace".

It was shortly after this that my mother's sister, Daphne, came to stay for a few weeks in the verandah flat; this of course wasn't being used now, in the absence of my grandparents.   I also had two uncles from this side of the family, Dennis who lived in Australia, and Jimmy who had just joined the army.   Daphne was married to a naval officer, but apparently the marriage hadn't worked out , and whilst waiting for the pending divorce, she had decided to 'take stock' for a while; where she was among friends and relatives.   The divorce was to be an amicable one on the grounds of incompatibility, but they were still, as they termed it, 'good friends'.   In the early spring of 1941 Lt-Cmdr.Nat Vaughn-Oliver, - my uncle Nat, who had just returned to the country, decided to spend a few days in Brighton and tie up any loose ends before the divorce to Daphne became absolute. During his short leave he had the use of a car, and on one of those days he drove my father, who was a very good friend of his, and my mother and me, to a favourite place of theirs, Telscombe village - just near Peacehaven and only four miles or so from Kemptown.   It was the first time I had seen this remote and unusual little village, which nestles in the South Downs not far from the sea, and in those days, boasted, no pub, no policeman, and not even anything that could be called a 'real' shop.   My mother liked to visit the church of St.Lawrence here, and some years before this, both my mother and father had been invited to visit the beautiful manor house, and whilst visiting there had walked the picturesque gardens - as had the likes of Rudyard Kipling, Charles Laughton and many more hallowed names.   The next day uncle Nat drove us to Barcombe Mills on the River Ouse - just north of Lewes.   We were all taken by the peacefulness and beauty of this place, and also its isolation, and, especially for me, the wildlife.   My father and uncle Nat spent their time there talking of fishing and about the sea trout that journeyed up to this part of the river each year to spawn.   They were both very keen fishermen, and in more peaceful times had often fished together. The next day he returned to his ship, and the war. I only saw him very rarely after this; in the years to come I read several of his published articles on fishing and the countryside he loved so much. He had told my father, during his leave, that his ideal life after the war was over, would be to have his own boat converted into a houseboat, which he would be able to move about from backwater to backwater in the quest of tranquility and fishing. Years later, in one of his articles, he wrote of 'nearly catching' one particularly large specimen after being awoken by the rod nearly being pulled out of his hands, whilst taking a nap while fishing from his houseboat on a quiet stretch of the River Adur. Uncle Nat was obviously not just a dreamer!

During her stay, Aunt Daphne relieved my, somewhat nerve shattered, mother, of some of her duties; this included taking Jill and me into Brighton now and again - including occasional visits to one of the town's main cinemas. She was what I can only describe as a 'smashing aunt', she was good looking and kind to a fault; she was something of a ditherbrain and a bit of a hopeless organizer - she exuded a general feeling of warmth to everyone, laughed a lot, and we all loved her dearly. She was also a very good ice skater, and before the war had appeared in ice shows - including the seasonal ones at the Brighton Ice Rink in West Street. When Daphne married again, quite quickly after the divorce, it was to someone totally different in his lifestyle, to the quiet, shy and thoughtful Nat Vaughn - Oliver.

My mother appreciated Daphne's help very much; in particular, because her health was beginning to fail - not seriously - but badly enough for her to visit the doctors; something she didn't like doing at all. My father was also having health problems. The stump of the leg that had been amputated, was not only causing him pain,but worst of all - as he put it - "the terrible twitching." The nerves, in what remained of the leg, would sometimes make it twitch violently, and whatever the doctor gave him to alleviate this - quite simply didn't work!

It was at this time that my mother started to take an interest in spiritualism.   She still attended the local church, St.Marks, and sometimes St.Wulfran's at Ovingdean, but she was interested in exploring all the possibilities of life after death!   It was through her visits to the spiritualst church that she met Mr.Campbell, a large man with a deep voice, who had spent many years in Canada and had a slight accent; he was a 'faith healer', and in particular, mother told us, 'a layer on of hands'. Mr.Campbell had apparently helped many people, in various stages of different illnesses, by laying his hands on the affected parts.   My father, having been told this, knew what was coming - and at first adamantly refused to let Mr.Campbell come anywhere near to "laying hands" on the stump - but eventually he conceded to my mother's common sense argument that, "It could do no harm and might do some good!"
Mr.Campbell called on us once a week at first, and my father, at first very sceptical that any good was coming from these sessions, - eventually had to agree, thankfully, that the 'twitching' had practically stopped, and from there on, looked forward to his visits.
  I also looked forward to them; I never witnessed any of the healing sessions - during those I was either out or in another part of the flat - but when he had finished each time, he would tell me stories about the Indians and their ways of life in North America and   Canada; a subject dear to his heart.   These true stories fascinated me; some were exciting, all of them were highly interesting, and I remember most of them to this day.
Mr.Campbell became a regular visitor and a very good friend to us for the next several years.

In April 1941 I was one of several new boys at Brighton College Junior school, Peter was also in this intake. On the first day of that first term, my parents accompanied me to a meeting with the head master, Mr. Stokes, and his wife, who was also the school dietician.   I was dressed in the school outfit of short grey trousers, grey herringbone jacket and long socks with purple and white markings, that came nearly up to the knees; also a cap with the same colours. For that term, we were under the charge of Miss.Allen, who was also in charge of the cubs. Those first days were very similar to kindergarten days, and we were gradually eased into new subjects, but for now the Latin verbs and French pronunciations were still some way away. There was always a threat of air raids at any time of course, and we soon got used to sheltering in the basement of our part of the college, Bristol House - where, we were told, we would be quite safe during the raids!

Being away from our parents for the first time during an air raid was particularly distressing to all us new boys, but we got used to it, and it seemed that, at that time, the day raids were not so frequent - it was the nights that the enemy were still mainly concentrating on. For my first term I stayed for school dinners, but after months of listening to my luridly exaggerated descriptions of how terrible these meals were; like a few other day boys who lived nearby, I was allowed to eat at home at mid-day. I would walk to and fro along the Eastern Road, never of course during an air raid, but if there had been any air raid activity earlier I would usually be met somewhere along the way. If the weather was bad however, I was given the money to bus both ways, but usually, if I thought I wasn't going to get completely soaked, I would run all the way there - or back - or both, and sometime later spend the money at the school tuck shop, just near the sports field.

It had by now become evident to Miss.Allan that I was no budding genius likely to take the academic world by storm, and I eventually found myself starting in the bottom class. The sporting side of things though were a different matter, and cricket, football, athletics and swimming, received my total dedication.

As we could no longer use the beaches, my mother now liked to take us for long walks on Sundays before lunch, if the weather was suitable. Quite often this entailed taking quite a large party of us, including my sister and some of her friends, me and some of mine - and usually one or two other mothers as well. On the first

49

Sunday after the term had begun, she and Bunty Ledgard, took a group of us for a walk to Ovingdean - this time going along the 'overcliff walk,' which could still be used by the public, and along which, from time to time, we passed sandbagged gun posts; all of which were manned and ready for any action that might come their way. We also went by the entrance gates to Roedean School - this had recently been taken over by H.M.S. Vernon as a training school, and now had two naval sentries standing outside. This impressive building is a well known land mark for channel shipping. Passing here we continued on the path to Ovingdean Gap; the beaches here were also no go areas and well 'barbwired' off from all but the military. Here also, is the site of another well known land mark - the art decor building of St.Dunstans, the foundation stone of which had only been laid as recently as 1937. This also had sentries guarding the entrance and was also taken over by H.M.S.Vernon. After Dunkirk, with the future looking bleak and invasion a real probability, it had been decided to evacuate everyone at this new building to 'Church Stretton,' a beautiful part of the country, ideally situated in the hills of Shropshire. In the magazine, 'St.Dunstans - a story of accomplishment,' it says, "many St.Dunstaners themselves worked in cival defence as air raid wardens, - roof spotters identifying aircraft by sound, and in the home guard." It is said that they were extremely adept at identifying aircraft by sound.

On continuing, we walked on up towards the church, passing hedgerows which we eagerly searched for nests - finding quite a few - nearly all with eggs in them. These were the nests of greenfinches, linnets and hedge sparrows, and under the watchful eye of my mother - we took no eggs, but one or two would be collectors were tempted! On our way home we passed St.Wulfran's church and the farmyard, where we stopped to look at the cows for a little while - then the Grange, and then made our way back over the downs, once again precariously going past the golfers, and eventually arriving home, windswept, a little tanned, and very hungry.

That afternoon Timmy had once again commandeered the highest climbable branch of 'our tree' - I had dared to go nearly a high as him; Peter and Michael were on branches a little lower down.   I noticed that Tim had wedged a flat piece of board on the foliage of a branch close to him; on that piece of board were a few unevenly rolled mudballs - made easier to make by the rain we had had the previous day.

"What are you going to do with those?" I naively asked him.

"Wait and see and I'll show you!" he replied, grinning widely. With that, holding firmly onto a branch with one hand, he picked up one of the mud balls with the other, and with a straight arm bowled it in the 'grenade throwing' style we had seen in war films at the pictures; it went up over the tree and towards the houses - it had been aimed to go into the basement area of a house where someone, who was always ticking us off, lived, but it turned out to be a very bad shot, and landed instead, on the 'workhouse' porch.

There was only one of the old men sitting on the step of the porch at the time; fortunately the 'mud bomb' - as Timmy called it - missed the old boy by about a yard, none the less a few bits of the mud got onto his trousers, and, letting out a few choice swear words, he brushed himself down but failed to see where this missile had come from; the thick foliage of the fir tree was effective in giving us quite a good hiding place.   After a while he turned and went into the house.   We all thought that this had been a rather funny prank, but unfortunately there was more to come.

"Come on David," Timmy said, "your turn next!"   I was very wary of having a go at this, but not wanting to lose face, and trying to prove that I was just as daring as Timmy, I picked up the nearest 'mud bomb' - and not bothering about the fact that the one I had taken seemed extremely solid, I hurled it in similar fashion, hopefully towards the basement that Timmy had been aiming at; however, I let go of it a bit late, and it went as straight as an arrow into the middle of the ground floor window of number twenty three

- two doors away from where Timmy's one had landed.   The hard ball of mud went straight through the window shattering it completely!   A year earlier the Hodgkins' family, from somewhere up north, had taken residence in the ground floor flat of this house.   Ian and Percy, the two sons of the family, I was to get to know quite well, as they were both already attending Brighton College junior school.   A few seconds after this disaster, with all of us now frozen with fear and staying where we were in the tree, the Hodgkins family started to appear on their doorstep.   Two boys, one girl, one mother, one grandmother - and then dressed in the uniform of a flight lieutenant - the father.   Unlike the old man from the workhouse, it hadn't taken them long to discover where this unprovoked attack had come from.   I was somewhat surprised to see that despite the damage caused by the mudbomb, the boys and the father were actually grinning, and in single file the whole family trooped into the garden and stood directly below our tree.

"Now then you youngsters -- you'd better all come down here." Mr. Hodgkins senior said in his north country accent. We immediately obeyed and were soon standing at the bottom of the tree surrounded by the entire Hodgkins family.   The boys and Mr.Hodgkins were still grinning; the ladies were all very solemn faced.   I didn't know whether to try to be polite and grin too - or perhaps just burst into tears and start saying how dreadfully sorry I was!   I decided to say nothing, and after a short silence Mr.Hodgkins said - "Now then - which one of you threw it?"   I sheepishly owned up.   "Ah yes," he said, "Master David Knowles isn't it -- I know your father lad!"

"Yes sir." I meekly replied.

"Well now tell me, Master David Knowles - and you others as well," he said, prodding each of us lightly on the chest with a pudgy finger, "I suppose that this means that not only do we have to take shelter from Herr Adolph Hitler and his 'bombs,' but now, it seems, we have to take cover from the home made variety, launched at us by our own side! I suppose you ARE on our side in this war." Mr.Hodgkins was still grinning, but looking straight at me.

"Yes sir," I replied again.

"Now tell me," he said to me, "was it a good shot?" I didn't know what to say, - so he continued, - "by that I mean, did you for some reason pick on our window on purpose, or did it get there by chance?"

I immediately owned up to it being - "a very bad shot! - An accident, I'm very sorry." I said, wishing the ground would swallow me up.

"Well, never mind lad," Mr. Hodgkins said - "it won't take too many years to pay for the window out of your pocket money - you'll have to come to some arrangement with your father about it, won't you? - But," he continued, "before you think of having another go at aerial warfare, I suggest that you buy a whistle - not quite as effective as a siren perhaps - but at least if you give it a good blast before you start bombing, it might just give us the opportunity to shut the shutters up and take cover!" We all laughed, and with that last remark as their parting shot, the Hodgkins family - all of them now grinning - trooped out of the garden and went back indoors.

Later on I confessed all that had happened to my father and he immediately went round to the Hodgkins to come to some arrangement about the window. That night my parents were invited to go round and have a drink or two or three with the genial Hodgkins, and I went to bed, somewhat sadder - a little wiser - and with my future financial prospects, like the window at number twenty three -- somewhat shattered.

CHAPTER FOUR.

A new found friend. – An accident. – A tragedy.

The water tank in the top gardens had become quite an attraction to us. In a year or so, newts would find their way mysteriously into the murky water - "probably brought there on birds feet," someone said. Homemade boats, some of them with sails, could be seen all round this newly built 'pond'. I made one which was definitely one of the more amateur constructions, it somehow made its way out to the middle, and then just stayed there until some boys we didn't know decided to try and sink it with lumps of chalk - these could now be found all over the place, after all the excavating. With anyone being able to get into these gardens now that the gates had been taken away, we found ourselves quite often in the company of children and youths from Whitehawk, Manor Farm and other nearby localities; some of these we tried to keep well clear of; sometimes, but not too often, there were drunken soldiers sleeping it off in the shade of some tree or bush, and we were careful to avoid these as well! Now and again though we made new acquaintances, adding a bit of variety to our lives, and some of these would remain friends for years to come. One of these new found friends was called Cyril, and over the years to come, he would be at the centre of several well remembered incidents. One of them occurred on the day we first met him. Some of the empty houses in the square and crescents were now becoming temporary billets for various military outfits, but the old preparatory school at 16 Lewes Crescent - which had had the basement reinforced as an air raid shelter in 1939 by John Gassen, who at the time was joint head master with John Arnold, was still empty. Under the guidance of our new found acquaintance, who was about a couple of years older than me, it was decided to explore this large empty building, getting in somehow via the basement - the idea was entirely Cyril's - but we were eager to be led; however we started having some misgivings, after Cyril had forced an entry through one of the basement windows. We hesitated for a few moments and then followed him into the house, and finding the bottom of a staircase - started to ascend it; however we soon became wary of going any further when Cyril told us that this was the sort of place that deserters from the forces were likely to hide in, and that they could be very dangerous, and might even kill us in order to avoid being given away - that is should we be unfortunate enough to discover any!

At about the same time that this piece of information was sinking in, we heard something or someone moving about on the floor above us. It was at this point that I felt that climbing trees was much more fun than climbing the stairs of empty houses that were probably full of murderers! Both Tim and Peter were of like minds, and Tim, usually the quickest off the mark, managed to blurt out - "I'm off!" - before descending the stairs at breakneck speed with me close on his heels, and Peter, bright red in the face and panting loudly, trying vainly to keep up with us - where Cyril was - we neither knew nor cared. 'In a heap' - we piled out of the still open basement window and practically flew up the area steps, only when we'd put about a hundred yards between ourselves and the old preparatory school, did we stop and look back. Peter, who had been about fifty yards behind Tim and me, eventually joined us, but was too puffed out to try and talk, and not seeing anyone else in view, I said, "where's Cyril?"

"He's probably being murdered!" Timmy said. But Cyril, who re-appeared a moment or two later, was still in the land of the living, and was now standing on the pavement outside the empty house, with arms akimbo and staring at us with some astonishment.

He later told us that the noise on the landing above us, had been made by a cat, which, like us, was probably exploring the place. After this we decided to be a little more careful when we went venturing where we shouldn't, and also to be extra wary about any more of Cyril's good ideas!

With all the rationing, things were difficult for everyone, but to make it even more so, it was announced that clothing would also be rationed - this coming into effect on June 1st 1941. This also included footwear - so families like ours - with fast growing children; especially with ones needing new school uniforms and replacements for anything they'd outgrown, feared that this would make things almost impossible; however, as it turned out, each person had an allowance of sixty six coupons for a year, and this turned out to be more than adequate, seeing you could get a childs jacket or pair of trousers for only six coupons. It was also pointed out to us that this rationing had been introduced, not to deprive us of our real needs, but to make more certain that everyone got their fair share of the country's goods. Also we were told that we could use these coupons anywhere, and did not have to register at one particular shop - as we did with our food rationing books. Items for children under four required no coupons - nor did boiler suits, hats and caps and all second hand clothing.

In those days we did practically all our shopping in Rock Street, and, Beeneys the grocers, Trethewey's the fishmongers, Webbs the greengrocers and Keilsdens the chemist's, kept us going with most of what we needed. Going to Trethewy's was a somewhat hit and miss affair owing to the unpredictable amount of fish available; sometimes, if the weather had been particularly bad, there was none, but usually there was enough for the shop to stay open for a couple of hours or so each week-day, and then it was a matter of first come first served. The shop I liked the most was 'the kiosk', a tiny building that stands on its own on the corner opposite St.Marks church - this kiosk is still there today. In those days, with sweets on the ration, we were allowed eight ounces each per month, but we frequently called into the kiosk if we had any pennies in our pockets - in case there were any broken bars of chocolate - which the proprietor would sell to whoever was first, without coupons.   Just along the road from here, and still on the Eastern Road, were another three shops, which included a grocer's, Farncombes the post office and stationary shop, and Glaskins, the bakers shop - run by two sisters who were as different as chalk and cheese - one being tall, the other being very short, the tall one very talkative, and the short one - hardly ever saying a word.

On June 5th, the news came through of the death of Kaiser Wilhelm.
"A pity," my father said, "that it wasn't Herr Hitler who had succumbed, with some of his henchmen thrown in for good measure!"
In those war time summers there was double British summer time, meaning that the clocks   would go ahead for two hours instead of one - consequently for quite a few weeks it didn't get dark until about eleven pm.   It seemed rather strange at first, but we soon got used to it, and my bed-time became a little later, just for a while - something that I didn't mind at all - although I still went to bed when it was fully bright outside.
The school holidays began in late July, and I remember finding that the last few days of my first term at 'prep' school were going very slowly, however, the longed for day duly arrived, and at mid-day Timmy, Peter and I walked back along the Eastern Road in anticipation of long summer days spent following many different pursuits.   The school was made up of day boys and boarders, and on that last morning of school, I had heard for the first time, the chants echoing in the dormitory corridors, -
"No more Latin, no more French,
No more sitting on a bench,
No more spiders in my bath,
Trying hard to make me laugh!"
'Etc.'

The time allocated for the summer holidays, for us, was generous, so on that day, the next term seemed like a lifetime away to me.

The barbed wire now stretched concertina style from one side of the bottom gardens to the other, thus, effectively cutting us off from the small slope down to the tunnel and many of our favourite play areas, including the much climbed oak tree that overhangs the path near the tunnel, and which is still there to this day.   The horseshoe though was still in 'bounds' -- this is a place shaped like a horseshoe which has seats inside and bushes on its outside, partly hiding a low stone built wall as its interior shaping.   We used to hide in the bushes here and eavesdrop on conversations by those using the seats - usually, blissfully unaware of our presence so close to them - that is they didn't know we were there until something was said that caused us to start laughing - which was quite often, and we would quickly escape from our concealment and 'disappear' into some other patch of shrubbery.   There were other trees we liked to climb here, including a walnut tree on the top east side of the gardens, from which, if the nuts looked large enough, and we picked them, and then peeled off their thick green outer skins - our fingers would stain as if we had been smoking heavily.   Unfortunately the walnut tree is no longer there.

Those summer holidays went quickly, but before going back to school we once again made our special trip over the downs to the blackberry patch for the big annual pick.   This time was to be more eventful however!   There were three grown ups, my mother, her friend Rhona, who had recovered from a longish spate of ill health, and Bunty Ledgard, Michael and Richard's mother.
My sister and a couple of her friends, and me with some of mine, made up a fair size party of us, and we all carried containers or baskets of varying sizes, which we were expected to 'nearly fill'.

Once again we passed the golfers, - even more numerous than before.   This time we had chosen a Saturday and again taken a picnic lunch with us.   Although on Saturdays we had started going to the Odeon cinema again, now that it was business as normal once more, we much preferred the fresh air outings such as this one. We arrived at the blackberry patch to find ourselves the only ones there so far that morning. My mother immediately encouraged us to start picking - "when you've filled your baskets," she said "we'll have the picnic lunch, then your times your own." We had invited Cyril to come with us that year - my mother had nicknamed him 'Tigger' from 'Winnie the Pooh' - because he always said he could do everything and liked everything, and this, we soon found out, was only until he tried it!

Once again the spiders webs adorned all the places that the best blackberries were to be found, and the fat little spiders defiantly tried to cling to the centre of their homes - unless a nervous and hesitant hand strayed too close, and then the little creature would quickly scuttle to the corner of a leaf and try to hide. When we had picked our quotas from the plentiful crop, we lazed on the grass and ate our picnic lunches and then went off to explore.

Cyril, after an incident when he had fallen out of a low branch of one of the trees in the top gardens, had shown a great reluctance for any more tree climbing; on this day however, encouraged by the nearness of an audience - which he hoped were watching him - he started to climb a dead tree; it was the only dead tree that there was there - and why he'd chosen it we couldn't guess, but this all happened before anyone had time to advise him not to climb it. When he was about ten feet from the ground, the inadequate looking branch that he was standing on, suddenly snapped, and Cyril fell like a lead weight to the ground - letting out a loud scream as he fell. He continued moaning and writhing around, until he found himself being comforted by my mother.

Unfortunately it was quickly discovered that he had probably broken his wrist, and also injured his shoulder for good measure.

After a short while he had calmed down, and, under the circumstances, now put on a particularly brave face, while my mother and the other ladies made much of a fuss of him and tried to make him as comfortable as possible. We all crowded round them watching what was going on, and when he eventually agreed he was alright to walk, we packed everything up and quickly proceeded on our way home.   At the golf club, after my mother had spoken to a gentleman she knew who worked there, a car lift was arranged to take Cyril, accompanied by my mother and Rhona, to the hospital, not too far away.   The outcome of all this was that Cyril had broken a bone in his wrist, and so needed to be put in plaster;   the shoulder had quickly been righted as well - apparantly to the accompaniment of a couple more loud yells from Cyril - who proudly showed us his plastered arm, when, bright as a button, he turned up in the gardens again the next day.   We, of course, all wrote on the plaster or drew a picture.   In the years to come we never saw Cyril attempt to climb a tree again!   As the grown ups and Jill and her friends hadn't completed their picking because of this incident, we went again the next weekend, this time with a smaller party, which didn't include Cyril.

The old men from the temporary workhouse were now able to use the top gardens, and while some of them took advantage of this, there were quite a few of them who never tried to set foot in them.   'Kingy', the one with the strange pipe, would regularly come out here after his lunch, if the weather was fine, and spend an hour or so snoring away on one of the small grassy banks left untouched by the excavations.   On a sunny day in late September that year, he was enjoying one of his siestas and had put his pipe, as he usually did, on the grass beside him.   When he woke up he found that the pipe was missing.   Quickly rising to his feet and mumbling away to himself, as well as voicing an occasional loud swear word, he searched for it unsuccessfully.   Several of us also searched high and low for it without success, and eventually the pipe was given up for lost or stolen!   Whether suspicion fell on any of us, we could only guess, but Kingy accused no one, and just complaining in general, eventually disappeared back indoors.
We felt sorry for him and had no idea who might have taken this

extraordinary pipe, and decided to carry on searching for a while longer.   A few minutes after Kingy had gone back indoors, I literally caught the thief of his pipe red handed - or, to be more correct - 'red pawed!' Doctor Longinato, a friend of my fathers who lived in Lewes Crescent, usually took his elderly Black Labrador dog, 'Negus' for his walks in the bottom gardens, but since the barbed wire had been put up, and a lot of his usual walk was now out of bounds, he occasionally walked up to the top square gardens, where he could even let Negus go off his lead for a while, in the bottom gardens, dogs had to be kept on leads.

After walking the dog round the square he had stopped for over half an hour, talking to some people who were also out walking their dog.   During my renewed search, I stopped to stroke Negus, and as I approached him he picked something up in his mouth from just in front of where he was laying - it was of course the pipe.   A little later I handed it back to a grateful Kingy at the workhouse; I didn't say anything about Negus, because Kingy was very 'anti' dog, and judging by the way dogs seemed to growl the moment he came anywhere near to them - the feelings were obviously mutual.

Another incident concerning this pipe happened on a warm sunny afternoon shortly afterwards.   Kingy had now started putting it in his jacket pocket, instead of on the grass, whilst he took his nap, and one afternoon he was discovered to be, not only asleep, but also on fire, with smoke coming from his burning pocket. After this he made sure of knocking the contents out before putting it away!

The affair of 'the body' also happened during that summer. One Sunday morning Peter and I were walking on the path towards out tree, when we discovered, to our horror, what looked like a dead body lying under a bush.   There seemed to be no breathing or movement at all coming from the 'dead man', he also had a funny colour and looked like - what we thought a dead body might look like.   "He's dead," I said to Peter, and panicking, we ran to tell the nearest grown ups, an elderly couple we knew slightly, who were walking nearby.   They came over to where the 'body' was, and, quickly ushering us away, confirmed our suspicions that this was indeed someone who looked to be dead. Before long a crowd began to gather and after about a quarter of an hour the police arrived, - then an ambulance. A small throng of officialdom now surrounded the 'body' and a stretcher was made ready. All of a sudden there was a bit of a commotion amongst the crowd, and the police and officials - all took a few steps backwards, in order to allow the body, as everyone was amazed to see, struggling to get on its feet. There was quite a bit of laughter among the police and ambulancemen, and eventually the bedraggled man tottered off out of the gardens and in the general direction of Arundel Road.- where we were told later, he lived. Apparently he had been on his way back home the previous night after leaving the pub, in a state of some inebriation, and thats the last he could remember. After this incident, I knew the meaning of the expression, "Dead Drunk!"

In early November, Cyril, with his wrist now out of plaster, instead of being thought of as an object of mild ridicule - now had the sympathy of us all. He had two sisters, one of whom, at the age of eighteen, was an usherette at one of the main cinemas in the town. We often used to see her walking past the square or coming to collect Cyril from the gardens. She was returning home by bus late one evening, after work, when there was an air raid - she had just stepped off the bus at Arundel Road, where she lived, when a piece of shrapnel from a bomb that had exploded nearby, entered her right temple and killed her instantly. This tragedy shook us all, and from then on we saw much less of Cyril, who we soon found out, was now being now being kept more closely under his heartbroken mother's vigilant watch, during those dangerous times.

I was now bcoming more aware of the cruelties of war and all types of thoughts were going through my mind. Fortunately time is a healer, especially in the mind of a child, but a death such as this one - of someone who's face you could easily visualise, someone you have even spoken to recently, even if it was just a casual "hello"- stays in the mind for a long time, and is something I shall never forget.

A few days after this another piece of bad news hit the headlines. H.M.S. Ark Royal had been sunk after being torpedoed by a U boat east of Gibralter in the Mediterranean. They had tried to take her in tow, but apparently the list had got very bad and she sank in the early morning of November 14th,1941. This sort of bad news, together with the air raids, and all the deprivations and restrictions, didn't exactly do much for morale at the time, and with the onset of winter and Christmas not far away, everything seemed rather bleak!   However, on December 7th the news that the Japanese had - without any declaration of war - attacked Pearl Harbor, meant that it was now inevitable that America would enter the war against - not only the Japanese, but also the Germans, who with the Japanese and Italians, formed the axis power.   Despite more bad news three days later, telling of the sinking of H.M.S.Prince of Wales and H.M.S. Repulse, off the coast of Malaya, there was a general feeling of not being so alone on this island of ours, and that the Japanese, in their murderous attack, had indeed awoken a sleeping giant - giving us a very strong and welcome ally - even if there was an ocean separating us.

On Christmas Eve with all the shopping done we eagerly awaited the early evening when once again we would sing our carols around the square and crescents.   We were expected at many of the places we called at - but this year there was one particular exception.   In the 1930's, an elderly German couple, who were Jewish and had found the Germany of that time a bad place to be, especially if Jewish, had come to live in a flat in Sussex Mansions in the square; the same building that Janine's and Michael's parents had flats in.   This shy, friendly and polite couple, who could speak just about enough English to get by, were always seen out together, never one of them on his or her own. They were obviously very devoted to one another and didn't seem to have any close friends.   It was suggested to us carol singers by Rosa Sammons, Janine's mother, that it would be a good idea if we sang outside their door this year as well, and that 'Silent Night', being of German origin, would be a good choice of carol.   We duly did this, and they came to the door and listened, even asking us to sing the first verse again - we gladly obliged - then wishing them a merry Christmas, left them shyly smiling at us as we continued on our way.

That Christmas and New Year passed quickly and quietly with not much in the way of enemy activity on the home front.   The news from the far east was that Hong Kong had fallen to the Japanese on Christmas Day, and the news in general from that quarter was that the armies of the land of the rising sun were advancing everywhere!

The new year came in with some very cold weather again, and during January there was a fair amount of snow.   The sledges that we had only tried out in the gardens in previous years,   we were now allowed to take to the downs near the golf club, and just above East Brighton Park.   With the snow not too thick on the ground and frozen solid after some quite severe frosts, we found that the steepest of the well used descents were too fast for us, and so, mainly used the smaller ones where the snow was a little thicker and not quite the texture of an ice rink, like the others.

We had been warned to be very careful on that first occasion and were more spectators than partakers in this thrilling sport.   We were amused to watch one boy sledging down one of the fastest descents on a large old tin tray; he did this very successfully and skilfully.   A bit later, a family arrived on the scene with a large and elaborately built sledge; they took it to the same run as the boy with the tin tray, but before any of the children of the family could use it, the father said he'd show them the way to do it!   He laid down flat on his stomach on the sledge and asked them to give him a push.   They did, and at an enormous speed, he whizzed off down the icy track, getting ever faster as he went down.   Before reaching the steepest bit near the bottom, he must have had second thoughts, and tried to manoeuvre the sledge into the thicker snow at the side of the run, to slow it down - this effort was unsuccessful and the man and the sledge ended up in a hedge that surrounded a small thicket, just above the playing field and about twenty yards further to the right of where he should have gone!   His family ran down the hill and eventually managed to help the prostrate father to his feet, and, putting an arm around his wife and a hand on the shoulder of the oldest boy, he limped off the field leaving the other two children to drag what remained of the sledge after them; they soon disappeared from view and our attention once again focused on the boy on the tin tray, expertly speeding down the same track again, for the umpteenth time!

The day before my father's birthday, in early February 1942, the news came through that the Japanese had landed on the Soloman Islands, and also on New Guinea.   This meant that if they were to make a firm foothold there, and completely overtake New Guinea, that Australia, like England, would have an enemy situated just across the water from them, and a very real threat.
My grandparents, who were still living in Cumberland, had been offered by their oldest son, our Uncle Dennis, to go and join him and his wife in Australia in early 1939, when things were beginning to look very bad in Europe. They had declined the offer, but a year later wished that they hadn't, now though, things were different again and they were glad they'd stayed in this country.
Australia, at that moment in time, looked to be the place not to be!

CHAPTER FIVE.

Imaginative games. – Indoor fireworks.

On February 9th, my fathers 51st birthday, it was announced that soap was to be rationed, an item of news that didn't exactly drive the 'William Brown's' of our crowd to the depths of despair.   In the winter, reading was quite high on our list of things to do on days when the weather was too bad to go out, and the Just William books by Richmal Crompton came out just about top of the ones that 'our crowd' preferred to read.   On the days when we could get out of doors at that time of the year, we mainly chose to play in the bottom gardens.   The iron railings surrounding all the gardens had now been taken away to be used for scrap to help in the war effort; but although the top gardens remained unfenced until after the war, the bottom gardens were now fenced off with chestnut palings, which had been supplied already interlaced with some wire netting, and this together with some newly adapted gates, was sufficient enough to keep these gardens open to key holders only.   At the end of the war we found out that the old railings had never been used for scrap - or anything!   This made the whole undertaking an expensive waste of time and somewhat annoying, when taking into consideration the urgency that had been stressed about how important it was for the war effort!

If the weather permitted it, and if we weren't at school, we would meet up at the horseshoe and then decide what we were going to do that particular day.   Although getting a little older, we still liked to play `gap games' in the spaces of grass, shrubbery and trees that hadn't been excluded to us by the barbed wire, and this was still quite a large area.   If we had seen a particularly good adventure or western film - one which had stuck in our minds - we would imitate the characters from these films and play out some game, usually along the lines of the film.   We also sometimes copied the characters from well known books, such as, 'Treasure Island', making sure that if we chose that particular story, whoever played the part of 'Long John Silver', was definitely not to 'overact' if my father happened to be in the gardens at the time!   One morning, when gathered at the horseshoe, Peter said, "how about having a 'Just William' game for a change - we've never played that one before." The idea was immediately agreed upon.

"Well it goes without saying who David's going to play!" Janine said, and my heart sank a bit when she said this. "The thing is who's going to play William?" she continued; we would probably have chosen Timmy, but he didn't like these 'childish' games much any more, and we were seeing just a bit less of him in any case.

"Let Michael play him," I begrudgingly said, and everyone quickly agreed.   The normally rather quiet Michael said, "I think Peter would make a good Douglas" - and that was agreed.

"Well, there's only one person you can be Janine," I said - trying to get my own back, "and that 's Violet Elizabeth Bott!"

Everyone laughed, except Janine, who said - "I'll play Violet Elizabeth Bott over my dead body, and in any case she lisps and I'm not lisping for anyone!

"You've got to play her, you're the only girl" I said.   But Janine was adamant - and it was Michael who suggested that perhaps a 'William' game wasn't such a good idea after all and we all agreed that we'd play something else; secretly I was very pleased about this, because as Janine very well knew - I absolutely hated being called 'Ginger'!

At number thirteen, the top flat was now empty; Julian Belfrage and his family had moved to pastures new.   Bruce Belfrage seldom read the news now on the radio - his particular place there having been taken over by a gentleman called Wilfred

Pickles.   There was a small conservatory built onto the roof at number 13 - it's gone now - but in those days it was quite an attraction to everyone.   I remember we once viewed an eclipse from there, and if you wanted to, you could step out of this glass construction and sunbathe on the roof on appropriate days.   Bruce Belfrage had apparently often slept in here as well; enjoying a celestial ceiling, but sometimes having to leave it very hastily when the siren sounded.   Sometimes we'd clamber out onto the roof, and if seeing a likely victim, such as one of the men from the 'workhouse', we'd shout out to him, at the same time as promptly disappearing from view - leaving him looking somewhat puzzled on the pavement below!

The verandah flat was still unoccupied, my grandparents deciding to stay in Penrith until the hostilities had quietened down.

From time to time I would invite a friend to play snooker with me here, taking great care not to tear the cloth, and never extending the invitation to play there on a Sunday! During that summer, my aunt Daphne came to stay in this flat again for a while.   Since her divorce, she had quickly remarried, and her new husband, Charles Gordon - a tall, quite handsome local man with a deep booming voice and regarded as a 'bit of a character' by those who knew him, had recently joined the Airborne Regiment as a private and he was still doing extensive training.   Just after she arrived I said to my mother that Aunt Daphne seemed to have got a lot fatter!   She laughed, and told me that Daphne was expecting a baby quite soon; she also went on to explain a bit more about the facts of life - thus forever dispelling the questionable 'old tale' - that a stork had delivered me by dropping me down the chimney pot!   I was pleased that she was with us again and hoped the outings down town and to the pictures might start again;   this though was not to be, because, as I was soon to find out, babies, even if they haven't arrived yet, come first, and also the new school term was just around the corner.

The summer term of 1942 marked the beginning of my second

year at Brighton College Junior school and I now found that I had to take homework back with me each day.   I had moved up a class, but my studies were certainly not going to get me anywhere - "unless I start pulling my socks up", as my form master had told me.   The sport though was a different kettle of fish, and I was doing quite well in most activities in that field.   Because of the double British summer time and because I was now a year older and had an hours 'prep' to do each evening, my bed-time was now extended to nine thirty p.m. Jill would usually stay up until about ten p.m. - and on Saturdays I would too.

On Saturday June 26th. just before my bed-time, I was about to put my pyjamas on when there was a sudden air raid; I don't remember hearing any siren, but I do remember hearing a lot of gunfire.   We stood frozen where we were for a few seconds and then with more gunfire - seemingly coming from all over the place - we hurriedly made our way down to the basement.   The raid carried on for a few minutes and then everything went quiet and before long we heard the welcome sound of the all clear. When we arrived upstairs we could see smoke and a big orange glow coming from where the gas works were.   My parents soon joined other spectators on the pavements of the square, and Jill and I were allowed to join them when they walked down to the corner to get a better view of what was going on in the direction of the gas works.
A mixture of smoke and ashes drifted over our heads and two fire engines sped past us to join the ones already on the scene, there were police and air raid wardens everywhere and more and more people started arriving outside their houses to get a better view.
We were told that two German aeroplanes - later confirmed as M.E 109's - had attacked Marine Gate, a large block of flats on the sea front, and also attacked the gas works;   hitting one gasometer, which promptly exploded after escaping gas had ignited.   We were later told the 'huge orange glow' from this could be seen from miles away, and it took the fire brigade until well after midnight to get this 'inferno' under control.   While all this had been going on a

69

woman dispatch rider had come off her motor bike practically at our feet, injuring herself quite badly; my mother was one of several people who tried to help her, but she wouldn't let anyone touch her until an ambulance arrived and took her to hospital. Eventually we went back indoors, but still watched from the window for a while.   Just before going to bed I could see the sky was still illuminated from the area of the gas works and there were still plenty of people watching from the pavements.

The next day we were told that Marine Gate had not been bombed but had come under heavy machine gun fire.   In the years to come there would be more attacks on this large block of flats - which was also something of a landmark - being on the sea front and in such a prominent position.   I knew of several boys at 'prep' school who had lived there before the war and all of them had moved away to similar accommodation in Hove, which was not quite in such an exposed setting.   There were some people who stayed on in these flats during the hostilities, but I have no record of any casualties there during that particular raid.

Just a few days before this, we had heard the news that Tobruk had fallen to the Germans, and although Hitler's invasion of the British Isles hadn't taken place;   what with air raids like this one and continuing bad news like that; the atmosphere on the home front was somewhat depressing! My parents admitted that because of all this, it would have been an ideal time to go to the farm in Surrey, but with Aunt Daphne expecting her baby within the next few weeks, this was now out of the question as far as my mother was concerned, and we were promised that we would definitely go for a holiday there the next spring, so, for the rest of that summer the gardens and the downs were our playgrounds and places of adventure.   On the hottest of days we would gaze longingly at the sea, whilst perched at the top of one of the trees.   The air raids continued, but perhaps not quite so frequently, and being woken up in the middle of the night - for the time being - had stopped.

In late September my aunt Daphne became the mother of a

nine pound baby boy, and my sister and I added another cousin to the fold, in the shape of Charles Gordon junior, who became the centre of everyones attention - except mine!

A month later there was at last some good news concerning the war; the battle of El Alameim had been won, and as this victory was celebrated, there was distinct optimism in the air that this could indeed be the turn of the tide!

In peace time, in the top gardens, there would always be a good firework diplay every November 5th, or the day before that if the fifth happened to fall on a Sunday. This was not an official or even professionally organised display - just a lot of different families, mainly from the square, letting off their fireworks together. I can remember one or two of these enjoyable evenings reasonably clearly, but of course during the war years the only firework displays were the ones we didn't want, and 'Guy Fawkes night' was a more or less a forgotten date. That year however was to be an exception, and on November 4th. Uncle Charles, back home on a short leave to see his new born son for the first time, presented Jill and me with a large mysterious package, remarking as he did so, "something I saw in London whilst passing through, and thought you might like!" We eagerly unwrapped this unexpected gift and were pleasantly surprised to find that it was a large box of indoor fireworks. Quite a rare thing to get in those days, but it had been pointed out to Uncle Charles that it was 'old stock,' so the results couldn't exactly be guaranteed. We decided to ignore that bit and after a little bit of wrangling, managed to get our parents permission to invite a few of our friends to come and watch an indoor display at 6pm the next day. At just after 6 o'clock the next evening, our sitting room was crammed to capacity with both children and parents eager to watch this 'unusual event'.

The only space that was left, was by the table near the front window, where my father 'dutifully' stood waiting to light the fireworks - having already made sure that all the blackout was

totally secure.   During the next hour we watched serpents of ash emerging from small pill shaped fireworks and even larger snake like objects appearing from bright green, conical shaped witches hats; every now and again a quick bright flare lit up the darkness from a Bengal light and in between times, sparklers were waved hither and thither, their holders trying to make imaginative patterns in the darkened room.   There were also other types of fireworks that were mostly strange to us - one or two of these didn't work - but the largest firework in the box, my father had saved until last, hoping that this would be the appropriate 'high spot' to end the display with; this was another conical shaped firework - but much larger than the first one, and was given the name; 'Fountain of Fiery Serpents'.   It turned out that he couldn't have picked a better one to end the display with, because on lighting it, it spurted out a large amount of bubbling greyish matter and then completely split asunder and filled the room with extremely acrid smoke and fumes!   Everyone started coughing and made a rush to the door for quick relief in the fresh air outside.   My mother told us later that she was wondering how long everyone would stay for after the fireworks were over, hoping it wouldn't be too long as she had other things to do - this sudden exodus however was beyond her wildest dreams, and, beside herself with laughter, she congratulated my father for some extremely clever, if accidental, manipulation!
We laughed with her and the next day were told that the others had all enjoyed the evening, and that the last part would be especially remembered.

At school during that Christmas term, the assistant headmaster, Mr.G.P.(Bundy) Burstow, gave one of his lantern slide lectures which he always made interesting for children of our ages with amusing anecdotes.   This particular lecture was about some famous buildings in Brighton - in particular in the Kemptown area - and also of course about the people who had lived in them. During this lecture I learned one particularly interesting piece of

information which I determined to pass on to Janine and the others the next time we were in the gardens together, and on a dry and windswept day in late November, when we were gathered at the horseshoe - raising my voice, I said dramatically - "you'll never guess what happened in these gardens in 1908!"
"What happened?" Peter said.

Waiting until I had everyone's attention, I pointed to the south westerly corner of Lewes Crescent and said "you see Fife House - well in 1908 King Edwards V11's oldest daughter, Princess Louise and her husband the Duke of Fife lived there, and the king who had been ill with bronchitis, came to stay with them so that he could convalesce in the sea air which would be good for him --- "
-- "I know" said Janine interrupting me and completely taking the wind out of my sails, "-- the gardens committee wrote to everyone who used the gardens, asking them not to do so during the time the king was here, so that he could have them all to himself - and that's what everyone did!" she said. "I've known that for years!" she added smugly.

I felt somewhat deflated, my important piece of information had fallen flat and apparantly Peter and I were the only ones who hadn't been told this particular piece of local history before - or if we had - we certainly hadn't taken it in!

On the day we broke up for the Christmas holidays my class were allowed out a few minutes before the others for some reason, and I found myself walking home alone.   I had just passed the entrance to St.Mary's Hall on the Eastern Road when I heard an aeroplane somewhere quite close to me, at the same time I also heard some gunfire.   A few seconds later I heard the roar of the aeroplane flying directly overhead and the almost deafening noise of the Bofors guns opening up on the seafront.   This frightened me, and I ran as quickly as I could across the road and into Glaskin's, the bakers, almost directly across the road from St.Marks church, and where I was known by the two lady owners.

The tallest one of the Glaskin sisters, a very kind and talkative lady, told me to come behind the counter and sit on the floor - actually under the counter!   I did this and she quickly joined me.

Fortunately this was just a quick 'sneak' raid and I was soon very pleased to extricate myself from my peculiar shelter and the now overtalkative Miss.Glaskin, who, just as I was about to go out of the door, called me back and told me I could have a free go in the penny lucky dip box, which was always to be found standing on the counter.   I hastily put my hand into the sawdust that hid the prizes - pulled some tiny object from its mysterious depths - said, "thank you very much" - and leaving the shop at full tilt, ran all the way home, arriving there unscathed, out of breath, and clutching a tiny celluloid doll with no clothes on!

I was soon to hear some more about that particular raid from a school friend of mine, Michael Webb, who lived at Rottingdean.
It was particularly fortunate that he had had a bus ride to make for his two mile journey home from Brighton College, because if he had arrived back at Rottingdean twenty minutes earlier it would have been at the same time that a German aeroplane had dropped its bombs on this village by the sea, and had then flown in a westerly direction over Kemptown, machine gunned some streets close to where I had been walking, and then flown off out to sea.
A policeman who had been on duty at the crossroads at Rottingdean was severely wounded and later died of those wounds.

Michael's father, Doctor Webb, a well known and well liked local pracitioner, found himself having a busier day than usual, and whilst attending the wounded, he thanked God that the raid hadn't come a bit later when his son was due to arrive back on the bus.
We later heard that this aircraft, probably a Dornier, had been shot down in the channel, but as far as I know, this was not confirmed.

With the festive season practically upon us, included in our Christmas mail that year was a card with just a few words on it from my Uncle Jimmy, my mothers younger brother.   This, apart from festive greetings was to say that he was quite well now, and had recovered from the jaundice he had gone down with a few months beforehand. The letter was posted from somewhere out in the middle east, where he was serving with the Desert Rats. Also in the Christmas mail that year was a parcel from Australia,which amongst other things, included some tins of delicious cheese; these very much helped to eke out the meagre ration of just two ounces per person a week.

That Christmas was a very quiet one for us, there was the usual carol singing, which once again went very well and this time provided even more tobacco and various odds and ends for the old men at the temporary 'workhouse'. There were also the usual rounds of small Christmas gatherings at each others houses,and, of course, the candles being lit on our tree at tea time on the big day - with many of our friends, as usual, attending that.

On a blustery day shortly after Christmas, my father, who didn't very often go to the pictures, because of the discomfort it caused him with his false leg in the cramped seats - made a rare exception and told us he was going to take us to the Savoy cinema to see the much talked about new film, "IN WHICH WE SERVE", which was now showing there for the week. He also said that before that we would have lunch out at Jimmy's Restaurant, a popular eating place, in Steine Street, just off the bottom of St.James Street. "A special after Christmas treat!" He told us. We enjoyed the outing very much, and the film - based on the true story of the sinking of H.M.S. Kelly, which Lord Mountbatten was captain of at the time - even though it was a propaganda film - was well done, and as my father put it - "a very good morale booster!"

The next day, another windy one, I met up with 'our gang' by the water tank in the top gardens. "You see how 'our tree' is swaying in the wind," I said to them, "well, if we climb up to the top branches and hold on tight, it'll be like being in a lifeboat in a rough sea!" I had been telling them all about the film I had seen the day before. Somewhat surprisingly, they all agreed to give it a go - even Janine, who I thought might be a bit dubious about it.

Eventually we found ourselves being swayed, precariously but enjoyably, near the top of the tree.   After a while the game seemed to run out of further ideas and it was at that point, when we were wondering what to do next, that we saw that Cyril had come into the gardens and was now standing a little way from the tree, near the water tank.   He was holding a very interesting looking model sailing boat.   This was quite a rare visit for Cyril, who nowadays used East Brighton Park as his playing area;   however this time it was obviously the water tank that was the main attraction, so that he could sail his new boat on it.

"What are you doing?" he called out to us.

"We're playing lifeboats". I shouted down to him and tried to tell him a bit about the film, hoping to be heard above the noise of the wind in the tree.

"I think you're all daft!" Cyril shouted back.

"Why's that." Janine said as loudly as she could.

"Because you haven't got any water underneath you!" Cyril shouted again.

"It seems like we have in this wind." I said, firmly defending my idea to play this game.

"-- Well I'm going to sail a real boat on real water," Cyril said, and added casually - "you can join me if you want." He then walked over to the side of the water tank and started to prepare to launch the yacht.   I felt like calling back to him that we could perfectly well watch from where we were, but thought better of it as I saw the others already beginning to climb down the tree - in any case my arms were aching from holding onto the branches so tightly.

Before long we'd all joined Cyril at the side of the water tank and each of us had a go at holding the handsomely built boat.   The wood that the hull was made from felt rather heavy to me, Michael agreed, but Cyril assured us that thats how the boat, made by an uncle of his, was supposed to be, and when he thought that the right moment had come - he pushed it out towards the middle of the water tank.   Everything seemed to go reasonably well at first, and the boat, a little bit sluggishly, made it's way out towards the centre of the tank; but then, a gust of wind blew it over on to its side, and quite quickly, on to a partly submerged branch that lay stationary in the water.   At this stage the heavy hull seemed to be sinking a bit, only the sails were still clearly visable, but hopelessly entangled in the twigs of the dead branch.

We chucked lumps of chalk and bits of brick to try and extricate it, but all our efforts failed miserably, and eventually, Cyril - like Noel Coward in 'In Which We Serve' - abandoned his ship and went home, a sadder and perhaps slightly wiser young man!

The winter of 1943 was milder than the three previous years, and the sledges only saw daylight on a couple of brief outings, in very light snow.

A week before school was due to start again, I met Timmy in the top gardens.   "Lets walk over to Queens Park and see if we can get a bottle of lemonade each off John West." Timmy suggested.   John, a school pal of ours, lived in a house just beside the Hooper Struve lemonade 'factory' which his father owned, and was in the Queens Park area of Brighton. Usually, when we visited him, he would take us over to the outside of the factory and knock on one of the windows, attracting the attention of one of the ladies working there - and on doing so - if it was just the three of us, hold three fingers up in the air, and within a couple of minutes a lady would come to the door with three bottles of lemonade.   The same performance was repeated on this particular day, and a few minutes later - having drunk them - we said cheerio to John and began the walk back home; mission completed!   We had got as far as the entrance to the sports field of St.Mary's Hall on the Eastern Road, when we heard voices coming from the field; we stopped, and peeping through a hole in the wall, we saw quite a large group of army officers and civilians; in deep discussion and looking 'very important'.   We watched for a few minutes and noticed that some of the officers were from the Canadian army.

On arriving back home I told my father about this incident, and a bit later I heard him telling mother about it; also saying that hearing this piece of news and judging from what he'd been told in the last few days, it sounded like something 'big' was afoot, and apparently Brighton was about to get a bit more involved in various troop movements for some unknown reason.   The following day we saw some activity was going on at St.Nicholas House, the section of St.Mary's Hall at the top of the square.   With all of us being of inquisitive natures, we enquired from a man doing some work on one of the windows there, whether anybody was coming to live there, and if so, "who?"   The man told us that the house would be occupied in the next few weeks - but just who was coming, he couldn't be sure, but said he thought it was something to do with the army.

In the second half of February this building, and many others that at that time were unoccupied, would become the billets for a regiment of the Canadian army, who for a time would become an important and enjoyable part of our lives.

Aerial photo taken approximately 1935 Sussex Square - Lewes Crescent and garden and slopes down to beaches.

Mother, Father, Jill and Me, Top gardens – Summer 1936.

Janine and Me – Top garden – 1936.
Father in the Bottom gardens.

St. Mary's Hall – in the days of gaslighting. But much as it is now.

Inside Odeon Cinema, Kemptown, Brighton, after bombing
September 14th 1940.

1.   Roedean School.

2. St Dunstans, Ovingdean.

If the Germans had known that H.M.S. Vernon had taken over
these two well known landmarks as special training schools during
the war – they would probably have specifically targeted them.

CHAPTER SIX

The Canadians – Surrey Interlude.

On September 1st 1942 the Lake Superior Regiment, originating in 1885 0n the shores of Lake Superior at a place now known as Thunder Bay, and better known then as the towns of Port Arthur and Fort William, arrived on the trade wharf at Glasgow. It was a beautiful early autumn day, which was in contrast to the dull wet weather they had been told to expect. Before long, when they were properly assembled again, they made tracks south to eventually end up in the beautiful countryside at Frensham in Surrey. They stopped there until February 19th., when in convoy, they moved to Brighton. The journey proved to be something of a nightmare for the quartermaster who found himself with scarcely enough vehicles to transport the large amount of troops and equipment to this famous resort by the sea, and this necessitated making a second journey for some of them, in order to bring three truck loads of live ammunition with them - none the less - they kept to the schedule and on February 19th. 1943, they arrived at Sussex Square and other nearby locations.

The arrival of this large force, with all its trucks, Brengun carriers, and other types of military transport, caused much speculation among the local residents. Earlier, back in Canada, there had been some disappointment on the part of the officers and men of the Lake Superior Regiment, during the early months of fighting in Europe, at the omission of being part of the first, second or third divisions of the Canadian army; but on June 10th 1940 came the news that the regiment was to be one of the constituent battalions of the newly authorised fourth Canadian division. In Brighton in 1943 the eighth Canadian infantry brigade was, according to its instructions, responsible for the defence of Brighton and surrounding area, but the Lake Superiors and the infantry regiments were there for training and not for garrison duty.

They were quickly billeted all around us in various empty houses and school buildings in the immediate vicinity. A and B companies were situated in the still empty main school building of St.Mary's Hall on the Eastern Road, not much more than a hundred yards or so from the square. C company were billeted in the square at another part of St.Mary's Hall, St.Nicholas House (now St.Hilary's house). Some of the soldiers occupied other vacant houses in the square, which were available at the time. D company took over the empty deaf and dumb school, also on the Eastern Road, and in a more easterly direction - but still only a hundred yards or so away from the square - Headquarters company were stationed at Arundel House in Arundel Terrace, and the battalion parade square was in the grounds of Brighton College.

In chapter eleven of 'IN THE FACE OF DANGER', a history of the Lake Superior Regiment by Lieut. Col. George F.Stanley, arriving at Brighton at the time is described as follows :-

"The new location was something of a contrast to what the men had known at Frensham. With its sandy beaches, its long piers, its Kings Road and its Marine Drive, and its absurd oriental pavillion erected by a dropsical George IV, Brighton was a town of new sights and interests with its multitude of pubs, its cinemas and its night clubs, it was a town of new entertainments and new temptations!"

Military vehicles were now parked all over the place, even tanks could be seen on the move from time to time, and the smart, tough looking soldiers, dressed in regulation khaki with a green flash just below the shoulders, seemed to be everywhere. At first no-one knew for sure the reason for their being there, but it was hoped that this was part of a spearhead for an attack on the continent, rather than an elaborate new defence from possibly still being invaded ourselves; it was felt however, that the latter was now no longer a real threat. The soldiers, were, in the main, civil and courteous and soon very much looked up to.

For us children every day was a potential birthday, and bars of chocolate and other sweets were quite generously handed around for a while. The parents of all of our group had told us in no uncertain terms that we were not to 'scrounge' - but we didn't need to - the soldiers seemed to have adequate supplies, including, I believe, parcels from Canada, and knowing of our austere rationing, they were very generous in giving out these most welcome gifts. Something that no-one minded us scrounging for though, came from the packets of cigarettes they nearly all smoked.

The most popular cigarettes with the Canadians at that time were called 'Sweet Caporal', and printed on the backs of the packets were aircraft recognition details; in other words, what an aeroplane looked like from head on, from underneath and from side view. This series covered all the aircraft involved in world war two at the time of printing - so there were plenty of them. Just about all the children that I knew collected them and it soon became quite a craze.

My father, as an ex-regular army officer, quickly made friends with some of these soldiers and quite often invited one or two of them in for a drink and a chat; mostly though they would have lengthy conversations if they met in the top gardens. We were quick to notice many young ladies visiting the area now, faces that we hadn't seen before, but the Canadian authorities didn't welcome this, and in any case there were always the dance halls and pubs for more obvious meeting places. One of the very quiet Canadians, a young officer I can only remember being called 'Freddie', was something of a scholar, - he often spoke to my father, trying to glean from him as much information as possible about Brighton and the surrounding areas. I remember a group of us, with Freddie and another officer, walking over the downs to Ovingdean; this was at my fathers suggestion, because Freddie had told him he particularly wanted to see the church there. Firstly though we showed them the grange and the farm buildings, but it was the churchyard that Freddie was rather impatiently waiting to see.

He seemed to spend forever just reading the gravestones, with us all waiting, also a little impatiently, to start the walk back home.

We later found out that his grandfather, an Englishman, was buried somewhere in the Brighton area, probably the outskirts, and that apart from his duties as a soldier, this posting to Brighton had become something of a pilgrimage for him in his quest of trying to find out where that may be. "Something like looking for a needle in a haystack". my mother said, but apparently he persevered until the regiment left Brighton, though unfortunately remained unsuccessful.

My parents, having promised Jill and me that we would spend the spring holidays at father's cousin's farm in Surrey, now started to put some plans together. It was eventually decided we would go on Saturday April 10th. and spend five weeks there, which would mean Jill and me losing the first three weeks of the summer term; something, I didn't mind about at all. My sister was given some school work she could take with her in the hope that this would help her not to get too far behind the rest of her class in certain subjects. I was to get some more 'tuition' from my mother, and was given a few school books to take with me to 'swat up' on, which included Latin and French. I was also told by Mr.Burstow that I would have to write an essay about life on the farm at the end of my extended holiday.

After we had broken up, we still had several days before the Surrey holiday, and these passed very quickly. On the afternoon before leaving off, I climbed 'our tree' for what would be the last time for quite a while.. I was soon joined by some of the others.

"I'll bet you're looking forward to tomorrow" - Janine said a little wistfully.

"Yes," I replied - "but I'll miss the gardens."

"Well" Timmy said "it's not for all that long."

"--Will you miss us?" Janine asked.

I thought about this for a few seconds and then said, "About as much as you'll miss me when you go to Wales!" - Not knowing why I'd said it, and diplomatically changing the subject, I said, "has anyone got any swaps today?" - I was now talking about our 'Sweet Caporal' card collections; on most days we would compare collections and see if anyone had any cards duplicated which they wanted to exchange for ones they hadn't got.

"I've got a spare Junkers 88" Peter said.   But there were no offers, - Junkers 88's seemed to be rather plentiful.   A few months back and that conversation would have been double Dutch to us - but now we were all enthusiasts.   A little later I said goodbye to all my friends, and feeling a little sad, but none the less excited, I went back indoors, and with mixed feelings, awaited the big day tomorrow.

The weather, on the whole, was kind to us the next morning, but typically for April there was a mixture of sunshine and showers, fortunately, more of the former.   We arrived at Brighton station with a trunk and several suitcases; two porters quickly latched themselves on to us until everything was safely installed on the train.   The first part of the journey was to Redhill, where we had to change trains.   At Redhill more porters helped us, and we got the next train to Dorking.   With all the luggage we had with us, my father had phoned his cousin saying that when we arrived at the station we would get a taxi to the farm, but cousin Grace, being a farmer, had a special petrol allowance and insisted on sending a car to meet us at Dorking station.   We duly arrived at this station, and Mr.Jones her gardener and occasional chauffeur, smartly dressed and wearing a suitable hat for the job, was there to meet us.   After introducing himself he busied about getting all the luggage on the roof rack and in the boot, and we were soon on our way to 'Bunts Place Farm', which lay between the villages of Bookham and Leigh. After Bookham we also passed through a village called Strood Green.   The journey took only about twenty minutes, and we noticed, on the way, typical signs of the war, such as pillboxes, and large concrete blocks which had been placed strategically in order to impede any tanks should there be an invasion; these had been put there at the beginning of the war. We arrived at the driveway of the farm and 'Jones', as he was used to being addressed, drove up the gravelled road to the house where Grace Corbett, father's cousin, a small, elderly and pleasant looking lady, wearing a light floral patterned summer dress, was waiting on the large alcoved porch. Two elderly maids dressed in starchily traditional black and white uniforms, stood beside her; they were Annie and Janie; they were cousin Gracie's 'faithful old retainers', and had been with her for a very long time.

The house was a large, rambling, picture book type of country residence, with something of the Tudor period about it. The highest windows were small and latticed and house martins nests could be seen in the eaves, with the birds darting to and fro and busily attending to these fascinating constructions. This momentarily reminded me of similar nests we sometimes saw at Ovingdean Grange. We were ushered inside by Annie and Janie, who kept bustling about us - eager to attend to whatever we needed. Before long we sat in the dining room, where, from the French windows, we could see a lawn and then a field with some cows grazing in it, and something that pleased me especially - large climbable looking trees, dotted about all over the place.

It had been decided that we would all have bedrooms on the first floor for the first couple of weeks. An attic bedroom was being prepared for Jill and me so that the room we were now using would be available for another guest who came to stay from time to time. On the west wing of the house, Annie and Janie had an apartment of their own. On the east wing, also with French windows which opened out onto the garden, was the library, and this large and comfortable room was to be our private sitting room.

There were books galore in here and I immediately noticed a shelf full of 'Pip, Squeak and Wilfred' annuals, the same that used to appear in the cartoon strip in the Daily Mirror, and I looked forward to looking at all of these.

The early afternoon was spent unpacking and exploring the house; a thunderstorm prevented us from going out until after tea, when Jill and I explored the farm. We first walked down a path leading to the kitchen garden, where vegetables, in plentiful varieties, were grown and were more than adequate in supplying the big house, some of cousin Grace's friends, and the two tied cottages on the farm. These cottages were occupied by the Jones family in one of them, and the 'cowmans' family, the Cook's, in the other. We passed by all types of trees, including, beech, oak, willow and various types of conifer, even finding the nest of a long tailed tit in a rambling privet bush. This was the first time I had seen one of these beautifully made, more or less oval nests. Fifty yards or so in front of the cottages was a small orchard, where, in the long grass - a dozen or so large bullocks were busily feeding. We weren't too sure about these creatures, and so refrained from exploring in there that day. We then came to a bottom meadow where a small herd of cows were grazing; there were two small barns here, one of them full of hay and the smallest of them with some straw in it. We then crossed a field that led up to the drive we had come up earlier. A bomb had fallen in this field in 1940; fortunately there had been no real damage to the house apart from a few cracked windows, but the huge hole the bomb had made had filled with water, and various types of vegetation grew around and in it now. "It had," as cousin Grace put it - "created a pond overnight, and I decided to leave it as it was!" I was fascinated to see newts swimming to the top of the water - some of them the great crested variety. We then walked through a large meadow on the east side of the farm, this was grazing land again, with large oak trees growing here and there, and a gate at one side of it where a small road ran past on its way to the village of Leigh, and eventually Reigate. The buses from Dorking came past here. Finally we looked over another fence onto another couple of fairly large fields, one of which had wheat sown in it; the plough lines could still be clearly seen. Lap-wings circled and landed over various parts of the field, giving out their gleeful cries of 'pee-wit' - we had never actually come across these birds before, but knew of them from books, and knew that they nested on the ground; so, in my minds eye, the field became full of smoothed out places scratched in the soil, probably containing well disguised eggs.

In the distance the mocking call of a cuckoo could be heard, and, proving that they often foraged for their food well inland, came the plaintive cries of seagulls. All this was music to our ears - as if a prelude for the days to come. Eventually, enthralled by all we had seen, we returned to the house and spent the evening in the library, searching through all the book shelves. From the next day it was arranged that we would have most of our meals in the library. On special occasions we would still have the occasional meal with cousin Grace. The farm provided us with fresh milk, eggs and early vegetables, but one thing that I didn't like, and everybody else liked very much, was the farm butter, it was home churned in the small dairy adjoining the house, and I found it too rich; "a luxury," everyone said, but not me! On our first night at 'Bunts Place' the heavens opened up with another violent thunder storm and I listened a little nervously whilst the rain beat heavily against the latticed windows, but we were cosily comfortable in our new surroundings, and after all, it wasn't an air raid.

In the days that followed I explored the farm and nearby areas thoroughly, that is when the elements allowed it; the weather remained typical for April and very showery. There were one or two more thunder storms with heavy rain - after which, the farm had that unmistakable smell of - 'the sweet and the rotten, unforgettable, unforgotten!' I discovered a wrens nest in the smallest of the barns and also a tree with a hole in it where a green woodpecker nested and often gaily chattered from somewhere amongst the foliage. I also found a moorhen's nest in the reeds of a small natural pond near the entrance to the largest grazing field. I managed to climb one or two of the smaller oak trees in this field, but the largest ones went too far up before the first branch, and I had to admit defeat; for someone my size they were impossible to climb without the help of a ladder. On the more rainy days we played monopoly, or chess or cards; we read a lot of course, and I especially enjoyed the Pip Squeak and Wilfred annuals. My extra tuition was not taken very seriously, either by mother or me, but Jill did get down to some real swatting up for an hour or so each morning.

On the first Sunday there we all somehow managed to squeeze into the car and Jones drove us to cousin Grace's church at Betchworth. Although my mother had been quite regular in her Sunday visits to church up until then, this was to be the only time we went to church with cousin Grace, and Sundays were left for other pastimes; mother though did explore other churches, not too far away.

On the next Sunday we walked to the Seven Stars, a typically quaint looking country pub in Leigh village. Jill and I were bought ginger beers here, I remember they were in stone bottles and we sat outside the pub to drink them whilst our parents made new acquaintances at the bar, drinking something a bit stronger.
A little later we walked back to the farm for lunch, the skies were aircraft free and mother said, "do you realize that we've been here for over a week and we haven't had one air raid!"

I met some of the local children, and became quite friendly with a couple of them, but in the main I was the boy from the 'big house', and whilst not ignored by most of them, was none the less, 'not of their group'. I found that I had the farm more or less to myself, but there was plenty to do to keep amused. Now and again we would go into Dorking, sometimes with Jones in the car when there was plenty of shopping to do, and at other times on the bus. I liked Dorking, but I can always remember seeing an ironmongers shop there with a large amount of its stock standing on the pavement outside it; amongst all this and also hanging outside the shop, were large bundles of rabbit snares, something I'm glad to say you rarely see nowadays, but in those austere days,

93

obviously used mainly to help eke out the meagre meat ration.

The river Mole ran by here and my father and I spent an afternoon on its banks near Bookham, vainly trying to fish for eels with some garden worms and some old tackle that had been unearthed at Bunts Place.

Jill and I, after a couple of weeks, had changed bedrooms to a smaller, cosier one on the top floor, and we had that part of the house to ourselves, apart from an occasional visit from mother.

Neither Janie's or Annie's rheumatically affected legs would allow them easily to get so far, and cousin Grace never went up there in any case - my father, of course, found it impossible.

On a Saturday evening a few days after we had transferred to our new quarters, Jill and I were lying on our beds reading; we had had a full day, including going with mother to Dorking, where, after a general browse around the shops, we had had lunch at the White Hart Hotel and then spent the afternoon at the pictures.

We were just getting ready to turn the light off when we heard voices, and also some unfamiliar sounds coming from the gravel driveway leading up to the house. The voices soon became more distinct and we heard a woman crying loudly. By now I was leaning out of the window trying to see what was going on, and was amazed to see a large horse towing a caravan. It was a bright starry night and I could make out that the horse, which was a brownish colour, had a long white blaze on its head. There was another horse and caravan behind this. I could also make out that there were about four or five people there and that there was an air of panic in the general talk between them. We heard a loud knocking at the door and then I noticed that Cook, the cowman, and Mr.Jones had now joined the throng at the door; I remember hearing Mr.Cook loudly enquiring -- "what's all this about then." - in an authoritative and none too friendly voice. At this stage, the door of the house opened and I heard my fathers voice, as well as cousin Grace's, and after a minute or two, everyone, including the woman, who was still moaning very loudly, disappeared into the house.   With curiosity getting the better of me, and against Jill's advice, I crept down the stairs and looking secretly through the banisters, tried to see what was going on on the ground floor - just near to the main entrance to the house.   I could make everything out very clearly and saw some swarthy looking gypsies gathered in the hall, as well as my parents and cousin Grace in her night attire.

Annie and Janie were standing nearby; similarly dressed, but with funny looking white linen night bonnets on their heads. Cook and Jones were standing passively and looking at a woman laying prostrate on the floor and bleeding heavily from a large ugly gash, which ran jaggedly down the side of her face.   I noticed that Annie and Janie were just standing there staring and holding hands, but cousin Grace and my mother were attending to this woman, and a cushion had been fetched for her head to rest on.   This whole scene disturbed me, and I quickly returned upstairs to our bedroom and tried to explain to Jill all that I had seen.   About twenty minutes later the police arrived and a few minutes after that, an ambulance.   For a short while everything went rather quiet; all I could hear was some talking going on, but I couldn't hear what was actually being said - although I could distinctly hear the horses breathing heavily, and snorting, while chewing at the grass on the side of driveway.   Eventually the injured woman was helped into the ambulance, one of the men went as well.   The rest of the gypsies soon went on their way, and once again we heard the wheels of the caravans making a crunching noise on the gravel as the large horses slowly pulled them behind them.   Before long the police also left;   then Jones and Cook   returned to their homes nearby, and at long last the night was silent, except for the bark of a fox coming from not too far away from the house, and a train whistling hauntingly in the distance.   Within a few minutes of everyone leaving, mother looked in on us, and seeing that we were obviously still wide awake - told us what had happened.

Apparently there was a small gypsy encampment of several caravans on a stretch of wasteland about a mile away - they had only been there for a few days.   The husband of the injured woman had earlier that day bought a second hand gramophone - the type that you wind up and play.   This had come complete with just one record - the Mills' Brothers' version of, 'A Paper Doll,' - a tune very frequently played on the wireless at that time.   The man's wife had started playing this record the moment the gramophone had been brought into the caravan, and had carried on playing it throughout the whole of the afternoon and evening - the record being the only one they,'d got!   Eventually, after an evening of drinking, a fight broke out, when, on being asked to stop playing the record, she had refused and obstinately carried on playing it; this had caused a row between the gypsies, and, in the ensuing melee, she had been badly cut by a broken bottle. Fearing further trouble, the husband and his brother had taken their families away from the encampment, hoping to get help at the first big house that they passed - which happened to be Bunts Place Farm. We later heard that no charges had been made by the police and that after being stitched up at hospital, the woman, insisting she was alright, had left with her husband and family for pastures new.

During that April, my mother, Jill and I, had all celebrated our birthdays, and on my one I received, amongst other things, a five shilling postal order from my godfather, Alec Chalmers. The Chalmers family lived at number forty seven Sussex Square and he was the oldest son; both he and the oldest sister, Sylvia, were very good and long standing friends of my parents. 'Uncle' Alec was now serving as an officer in The Royal Gloucestershire Regiment, and was shortly to be moving quarters from Winchester to the Duke of Argyll's estate in south west Scotland, for combined operations with the navy, and, as we found out later on, for preparations for D-Day - just over a year later.   Sylvia Chalmers, had been my nanny when I was very small and had spent many hours pushing me in my pram around Sussex Square gardens; this had made it possible for our mother to accompany father in the car in his job as a representative for the building material firm

J.J.G.Saunders, which was Brighton based.   This job had been found for him by his well known 'cricketing' uncle, W.L.Knowles, the secretary of Sussex County Cricket Club who had a connection with this firm. He travelled throughout the south east.   Eventually, because of these journeys with him, she was able to take over after he had had his leg amputated and could no longer drive.   Sylvia, was later to become a much more important part of our lives.

On a Saturday night at the beginning of May there was an air raid, and from our bedroom window we could see searchlights beaming up into the sky and hear guns going off from all around us - but fairly distant.   We hurried downstairs and sheltered in the hallway until the all clear went.   This was the only time we had to do this during our stay in Surrey.   A bit later the phone went and one of cousin Grace's nearby friends, after enquiring that all was alright at Bunts Place, informed her that a German aeroplane had been shot down and had crashed not far from them, and less than a couple of miles from us.   The next morning,on our Sunday walk, we chose a different direction to our usual one, in order to find where the crash had been.   We eventually found it in a woodland area, now guarded by the police.   There were also several other people there, who like us were curious to have a look.   Had my mother known that we would smell the strange smell of burning flesh at this horrific scene, she would never have taken us there.
The crashing ME 110, burning furiously, had cut a swathe through the trees and finished up in pieces all over the place - with some of what was left of the pilot, ending up in one of the trees.   While we were there we could see wisps of smoke still coming from various parts of the woods, and the smell was a sickly sweet one, and unforgettable in a macabre sort of way. We walked back to the farm, shocked, saddened, -and not very talkative!

A few days before the end of our holiday I was sitting by the 'pond' created by the bomb at the beginning of the war.   I was fishing for newts with a piece of old fishing line with a worm tied to the end of it - no hook - just that!   The newts, if they bit the worm, would sometimes hold on to it, and, 'hey presto' - a quick pull and you'd probably caught one!   I'd already got a couple of the great crested variety swimming around in a large jar which I had beside me, when I was intrigued to see a snake lying curled up in the sun on some nearby dry bracken.   I had no fear of snakes at all; I had once kept a couple of slow worms as pets for a while, and thinking that this was a grass snake, I picked it up, holding it carefully just below the head; just in case I was wrong in my identification of it.   At that time, for some reason, I was quite sure that adders had a yellow streak just near their heads - and this one hadn't.   I took the snake back to the house with me and put it in a box with some grass in it, under my bed.   I remembered that there was a book about British animals among the many books in the library, so I looked it up.   Within minutes, I was very carefully carrying the box back to the field where the pond was.   I emptied the snake out where I had found it on the dead bracken and it lost no time in slithering off into the long grass - the black diamond pattern on its back showing up clearly, like the picture I had seen in the book - that it was an adder!   Realising that my sister would not be the only one who wouldn't be too pleased if she found out about this - I decided not to tell anyone about it - but I felt pleased with myself that I had handled it and lived 'not' to tell the tale!

A couple of days before we were due to return home, cousin Grace told us we would be welcome to come back at any time, and it was tentatively arranged that we would come back for another holiday the following year; this time making it for the summer holidays and probably coming at the end of July.

The next morning, after saying our goodbyes to Annie and Janie and cousin Grace, we were driven by Jones to Dorking station during yet another thunder storm, and a couple of hours later arrived at Brighton station to the accompaniment of more thunder and lightning and heavy rain.   By the time we arrived back at Sussex Square though, the sun was shining brightly again, and after quickly changing into some older clothes, I was allowed to go out to the gardens. After having a good look round the bottom gardens I returned to the top ones, and very soon climbed to the top of 'our fir tree,' where I spent a few minutes taking in the familiar view of the sea again.

The Canadian lorries and various other vehicles, now completely surrounded the square - all of them parked on the road just beside the gardens - and not by the pavements. Some of the soldiers that I knew spoke to me and enquired about where I'd been. One of them handed me a dozen or so Sweet Caporal cards which he'd been saving especially for me - some of them I had already got - but some of them I hadn't, and this was a treasured gift.

A little later Janine arrived home from school, Michael of course was still at boarding school, and Peter always had to do his homework before he was allowed out. We climbed our tree again and I was in the middle of telling Janine about our holiday when we noticed a strange looking small aeroplane flying quite high overhead - we couldn't make out the markings however and thought no more of it. I was about to carry on from where I'd left off, when we felt the first spots of rain of another squally thunder storm which was looming overhead, and we quickly made our way to Janine's flat - where I carried on relating about our holiday - with the added audience of Yvonne and Mrs.Sammons.

That night I reflected on the past few weeks and decided that I no longer wanted to be a pilot, or an England cricketer or footballer, or even a great explorer - I had now become somewhat more modest in my ambitions, and had resolutely decided that it was a farmers life for me!

CHAPTER SEVEN

Some Royal arrivals. – Under observation?

I began school again on Monday 17th.May and was soon back into the routine of things.   After school, in the early evening, I met Peter and Janine in the top gardens. Peter had been allowed by his father, who was at home on a few days leave, to borrow his very powerful binoculars.   We decided to climb to the top of 'our tree' and see what we could see with them; this time even Janine climbed up a bit further than usual, but still wouldn't venture just those few feet further to get to as high up as me.   I had a panoramic view of the channel and whilst I was looking through the glasses I got quite a good view of some warlike looking ship on the horizon, but couldn't identify what sort of craft it was.   Thanks to the Sweet Caporal cards, my aircraft recognition was good, but ships were a totally different matter, and I thought it would be a good idea if they started doing warships as well.

"DAVID! -- for goodness sake be careful with those glasses!" Peter anxiously shouted - startling me and bringing me out of my daydreams.

"It's alright I'm, holding them tightly." I said, making even more sure by putting the strap round my neck as I was supposed to have done in the first place.   "– Make sure you don't hang yourself!" Janine said sarcastically; impatiently holding her hand out for a go with the glasses.   I kept her waiting for another couple of minutes and then handed them to her.   She'd only been looking out to sea with them for a few seconds when we heard the sound of an aeroplane approaching;   this time though, with an unfamiliar engine sound, but when it came into view we recognised that it was a Sunderland flying boat; it was flying close inshore and going in an easterly direction.

100

"Give us the glasses, quick Jan." I ordered, stretching out my hand, but Janine was having none of that - and holding firmly onto the binoculars, watched the flying boat until it disappeared from view. "These glasses are absolutely smashing, I could even see the pilot in it!" she looked gloatingly at me as she said it.   I felt a bit jealous, but didn't say anything, although I thought that it was typical that it would be her holding the glasses just as the Sunderland went past.   This incident was quickly forgotten when Janine, urgently 'half whispered' - "David, you'd better get down the tree a bit, your fathers just coming in the gate and you'll be for it if he sees you right at the top again."   I looked, and saw he was carrying his deck chair in one hand and walking stick and paper in the other, and making his way over to where 'Blackie,' one of the Canadian soldiers we knew, was sitting on the grass just below where we were.   I quickly climbed down to where the others were, and before long, seeing that my father was reading something to Blackie from the paper, we climbed down and sat on the grass near to them, and tried to overhear what he was reading out.   He was talking about a headline in the Argus which told of the big R.A.F. raid on the Great Dams of Germany.

"It's made 120,000 homeless!" he said, "and the death toll is at 4,000 and still rising!"   Their conversation carried on on the same subject and we soon tired of listening and found something else to do.

That particular raid was of course the famous 'Dambusters' raid.   Many years later, with my wife and our three sons, we went camping at Reculver on the Kent coast near to Herne Bay;   this was where they had had the trial runs for the bouncing bombs they used on the raid.   These trials were done quite close inshore. The 'practice' bombs didn't contain explosive charges and were filled with something which assimilated the weight for dropping and bouncing correctly.   I still have a family photograph taken on that camping holiday, showing us all sitting on and around one of these trial bombs in a field just near the well known land mark of

Reculver Towers.

The weather in that part of May 1943 had been particularly pleasant, with plenty of hot sunshine and many people took advantage of this, including quite a few of the Canadians billeted in the square, who, when they could find the time, sunbathed on the grassy verges that still remained around the water tank.   They also spent quite some time instructing some of us in the finer arts of throwing horseshoes to land - 'hopefully' - around a metal pin, which was the target and was placed a reasonable throwing distance away.   Some of us became fairly good at this.   They had made use of a stretch of ground just near the largest of the fir trees. I believe they called this game 'Ringers.'   Also during this fine weather we watched them take part in various exercises and parades, - one of these in particular is mentioned in 'IN THE FACE OF DANGER,' an extract for that time says, '-- on May 19th came H.R.H.The Duke of Gloucester to witness a demonstration of tank warfare put on by the Canadian Grenadier Guards.   He could not see very much of the exercise because of the dust the tanks threw up in the very dry weather,but he did see the sunburned faces of the Lake Superiors as they lined the route along which he travelled.   The Duke could hardly have been aware of the fact, that these were the first cases of sunburn in the battalion since the days of the long march from Ottawa to Vaudreuil back in 1941.'   This was referring to a one hundred mile, five day march the regiment had had to undertake as they moved in an easterly direction from Ottawa to eventually board the coaches of the Canadian national railways at Vaudreuil for their journey to Nova Scotia, and later on, embarkation to England.

On the Saturday afternoon of that week it had been decided that there would be no visit to the Odeon cinema, but in the evening Peter and I walked along the Eastern Road to Brighton college, and were amongst some of the boys from the junior school; mainly boarders, who attended a showing of the film Henry the Eighth, put on by the senior school cinematograph society.

This was our first time of attending one of their films.   In replying to a letter of mine enquiring about films shown by the society during those war years, as a reminder to me for this book, 'Christopher Apps', the Brighton College junior school archivist, and an old boy of both the old preparatory school and the senior school, writes; "I eventually became secretary for the film society and booked films from 'Ranks' for weekly showings in the music room next to the chapel.   I was also an operator of the 'Bell and Howell' projector in the box under the staging in the music room, now removed.   Most of the boarders attended and it could be hazardous if your selection didn't come up to standard!"

I remember those special evenings very well, particularly the hard wooden step-like seats of that small auditorium.   On future cinematograph Saturday evenings after this, Peter took a car rug with him for us to sit on.   On that first visit we watched Charles Laughton as Henry the Eighth marry his selection of wives, and, whilst eating, chuck a few chicken legs over his shoulder - all this in between a couple of projector break downs that were loudly booed by the audience.   One thing I 'm sure of is that the projectionist, in his rather thankless job, must have worked very hard indeed, and I'm pretty certain also that there weren't many in that audience who envied him his job.

With the Canadians well settled into various parts of the town by now, especially the ones in the square, we were on christian name and nickname terms with many of them, also quite a few romances had begun, and courting couples could now quite often be seen in the top gardens - consequently, our 'younger group' found ourselves having to spend less time there and more time in the bottom gardens - our parents thus hoping we wouldn't stumble across any couples getting over passionate in some of the more concealed of our playing areas that remained untouched by the installing of the water tank.

With Michael at boarding school and Timmy usually seeking

slightly more mature company, our diminishing numbers were quickly made up by new faces as well as familiar ones now old enough to join us without parental accompaniment; the twins, Barry and Jill Power, who lived a couple of doors away from number thirteen, and were about two years younger than me, joined us quite frequently, as did Yvonne, Janine's younger sister. Now and again we still saw Cyril, and also now and again Brenda Bassett joined us with a couple of her friends. On getting that little bit older, we phased out the gap games and took to more sporting activities, such as cricket, football and rounders. Sometimes, especially while playing cricket, we were looked upon with disapproval by some of the residents who felt it their duty to keep the gardens from being maltreated in any way. Cricket balls, or even the stumps, would sometimes be 'confiscated' by an irate garden protector. One titled gentleman became quite a scourge to us; he lived in a verandah flat that overlooked our main cricketing lawn, and if he happened to be home at the time that we were playing there - and saw us, he would very quickly come into the gardens and try to confiscate any of our sporting equipment that he could lay his hands on. Firmly holding onto whatever equipment we had, and keeping our distance from him, we would argue, reasonably politely, against his way of thinking. Strictly speaking though, ball games other than catch, rounders or French cricket, were very much discouraged, and even those games we could play, had to be played with a tennis ball or something similarly soft. There were, however, some residents who actually encouraged us in our sporting pursuits, but we always watched out carefully for those we labelled 'enemies,' and in particular for the titled gentleman who we had secretly, nick-named "Sir Adolf." Ham the head gardener had recently left for a job with the forestry commission, and this left the mild mannered and pleasant 'Fryer' in sole charge. This pleased us very much as he was the one gardener we got on very well with. His sympathetic views of where we could play, were in our favour as long as we

104

made sure to be careful about treading on flower beds if we had to retrieve a ball - and never of course carelessly damage anything.

The trees were still well climbed, and it wasn't only the age groups such as my sisters or ours, who enjoyed this pastime. We once watched some amazing feats of agility by one of the Canadian soldiers, who, rapidly climbed to the top of the largest and most difficult to climb of the four fir trees, and then descended even more quickly, in monkey like fashion to the ground. This athletic man told us not to try to copy him though, and also told us that you could see trees like this one - and many much larger ones - where he lived in Canada, and described his home countryside as 'rugged and beautiful'.

There now seemed to be more of all types of military vehicles all over the place, including tanks on some sort of manoeuvres. Many of the tanks were based at Ovingdean where they had taken over the buildings and fairly extensive grounds of what had been Ovingdean Manor Preparatory School before the war had broken out. It was later found out that they were to be part of a special big exercise which was soon to take place; however the fourth division of the Canadian army, which included the Lake Superiors were considered still to be in need of further training before taking part in this exercise, consequently the regimental training programme was stepped up considerably in order to bring the troops up to scratch with the other divisions. This big exercise was called "SPARTAN", and was described in the Times as, "the greatest offensive exercise ever staged in the history of these Islands." One part of the training that the Lake Superiors took part in for this exercise, was some landing craft practice on a small lake deep in the beautiful Sussex counrtyside at Piltdown - not far from where the famous 'Piltdown Man hoax' had taken place. I remember my father saying to us that from the moment he had heard about the landing craft exercises he was confident that these manoeuvres were the build up for the invasion of the continent, but that what he couldn't guess of course was how soon that might take place. "Hopefully," he said "it's reasonably imminent!"   It was still widely thought that the invasion would embark from the south east corner of England, in other words the part nearest to the continent; but then again the most heavily defended area would be around Calais, and so the speculation continued.   The worst part of these army exercises was the way the tank tracks churned up some of the roads, but this was a small price to pay so that these men had at their hands all the facilities they required for such manoeuvres before the big day dawned.

On the following Sunday, May 23rd., I spotted a   small aeroplane similar to the one I had seen from the top of 'our tree' on the day I returned from Surrey; I told my father about this.

"It   could have been a German spotter plane," he said - "perhaps taking photographs - in which case we can probably expect to get some more air raids; especially with all these army vehicles everywhere, providing an actual target for them, so the next time you hear the siren go, buck your ideas up and get to shelter more quickly than you have the last few times!" In these latter stages of the war, whilst we did take shelter each time we heard the siren; unless we actually heard aeroplanes, or gunfire, or bombs - we tended to take our time - unlike the early days when we would race to take cover at the sound of the first wail of the siren.

The day after this, in a conversation with a couple of the officers of the Lake Superiors, my father told them of his theory about the spotter planes probably photographing their vehicles, and probably including the tanks, when on the move. These tanks, when stationary at Ovingdean Hall, were parked under the trees, more or less out of sight of reconnaissance planes; the concrete blocks that were specially made for them to park on, are still there to this day.   In replying to my father, they told him they were well aware that they were under scrutinization by the enemy, and that there wasn't much more that they could do in the way of concealment than they were doing already - such as parking under trees where possible, like they were also doing under the trees that hung over the road from the top gardens.   They also reminded him of one of Lord Haw Haw's broadcasts, when he had announced that "German planes would make it 'HOT' for Worthington's circus!"   -- Worthington being the General commanding the Canadian soldiers.   There had been quite a few air raids whilst the Canadians had been stationed near to us and a passage from 'In The Face of Danger' goes as follows:

"The Brighton stay was not all a matter of work and games. Situated as it was on the south coast of England within a few minutes flying distance of the continent, the town was exposed to frequent hit and run raids by German fighter bombers.   It was a simple matter for planes to speed low across the channel, their wings almost touching the water, then to swoop upwards over the town, to loose their bombs, fire a few bursts from their machine guns, and then hurry away again before the defending planes could take to the air.   During March and April there were several alerts in Brighton.   There were some casualties, but none among the Canadian soldiers stationed in the neighbourhood.   On April 29th. Private C.P.Repp of C company emptied his rifle at a speeding raider. His flying bullets may not have come any nearer their objective than did the shots fired by the cooks and clerks still endeavouring to qualify on the range, but at least he could claim the distinction of being the first Lake Superior to fire a shot at the enemy!"

Although there had been some bad air raids with further loss of life and casualties, including a direct hit on a hotel on another coastal town, not too far away from us; at lunch time on Sunday 23rd. May, a warm early summer's day, there were deck chairs out in all the favoured places that were sheltered from the sea breezes in the bottom gardens.   Janine, Peter and I were lounging around on the lawn just in front of the broken sun dial near the horseshoe.

"You see the house next door to where I live," Peter said pointing to number 13 Lewes Crescent, and where the crescent and the square joined up, "well," Peter continued, "in the last couple of days some Indian Princes and Princesses have moved into there!"   On looking more closely Janine and I could see the darker looking faces of some men on the verandah of the house, and also saw that they were wearing turbans.

"My mother said that it took several furniture vans to deliver all their stuff, and that they're from a part of India thats in danger of being invaded by the Japanese, so they decided to come to England" Peter said.

"Why did they choose Brighton?" Janine asked.

"That's what my mother would like to know." Peter said.

We soon became quite friendly with some of these new 'neighbours' of ours, who seemed to have an enormous family; but of course some of the people we saw, coming and going, were servants. The main family though, were made up of the Maharajah and the Maharanee, the two princesses, who in their flowing robes looked very beautiful, and the two princes - both perhaps just a bit older than my sister, and who quickly joined in in the activities of their age groups in the square and also had plenty of time for us younger ones - including occasionally playing cricket with us - they were called Nikki and Chota.

     "When I was in Surrey," I said, "we went to see a film with that Indian actor in it - you know the one I mean - Sabu."

"What was the film called?" Peter asked.

"Arabian Nights" I answered, and added, "but I still think 'The Thief of Baghdad' was much better, and he was in that as well."

"I remember that one," Peter said, "that was where he went on that flying carpet, wasn't it?"   The subject about Indians soon changed, but none the less, we were more than a little intrigued to have some 'actual royalty' living just near us.

     "I wish we could still get to the beaches," I said, "I could just do with a swim today."

     "Wouldn't the water still be too cold?" Peter said

     "Yes I suppose it would." I agreed.

     "It wouldn't be all that bad." Janine said, and I remembered from pre-war days that she seemed to be able to stay in the water, without getting too cold - certainly longer than I could.

"There is a place where you can still swim in real sea water not too far from here." I said

"Where's that?" Janine asked.

"We've got some friends who live at South Lancing and they sometimes go to a place on the River Adur where it's tidal and swim there, - but only at high tide." I said.

"Why's that?" Peter asked.

"Because if you go when the water's low, you have to walk through all the mud; but that's always covered up when the tide's high;" I replied – " in any case, Edie Whitehead - my mother's friend, is going to arrange for a picnic there in the summer holidays."

"Are you going to invite us?" Janine asked.

"--Well, - we usually do when we go on picnics." I replied pointedly.

"How do you get there?" Janine persisted.

"By bus from Poole Valley - it's on a part of the river at North Lancing, not far from Lancing College," I answered her. " - mind you, my mother was told, that when we get off the bus we'll have to walk down a small country road for about three quarters of a mile to get to the right place."

"Mummy said there aren't any sign posts on the country roads nowadays, so, unless you know exactly where you're going, you can easily get lost!" Janine said.

"Why's that?" Peter asked, looking puzzled.

"Because if the Germans invade us, and they can't find any sign posts they won't know where they're going will they!" Janine said.

I also added for her " - and if they ask the way it'll probably be in German - so we won't understand what they're talking about in any case."

"It all sounds daft to me." Peter said.

"It's not really," I said "because it'll mean that they can't read their maps properly, and that will slow them down, and that's the whole point of it! -- in any case my father said that the Germans probably won't invade us now." I added.

"We're still getting air raids." Janine said, "so how does he know?"

"He doesn't," I said, - "but air raids are different!"   We changed the subject - air raids were a subject we weren't too keen to talk about much.

Apart from the sign posts that the authorities had taken away from the roads, the press were also being careful not to give actual place names away in their reports of enemy air raids on this country - in other words if Brighton or Eastbourne or Hastings had had an air raid that had been bad enough to warrant reporting - then it would say that there had been a raid on a 'south east coast town'.   The following report in the Evening Argus is an example of this, and it also gives weight to the possibility that the Luftwaffe were now specifically targeting areas along the coast where there was a lot of military activity. Concerning the raids on Sunday 23rd. of May the Argus says:

"Four out of five F.W.190's brought down during Sunday's lunch time raid on three coast towns were destroyed by A.A.gun fire.The attacks were delivered simultaneously on two widely separated parts of the coast, -- a new departure in the Luftwaffe tactics.

Light A.A.guns in a south east coast town shot down two of the fighter bombers into the sea. Further along the coast a third was shot down by Bofors gunners and the fourth had its tail blown off by one of our fighters."

It was encouraging to know that our defences were having their successes, but these new types of raids were very worrying to everyone - especially the military of course.

Two days later, on Tuesday May 25th, Brighton was to suffer its most devastating air raid - one that would go in the history books and also add weight to the theory that the large build up of military vehicles all around us were indeed something specific for the Luftwaffe to aim at, and, might just be the real build up for an invasion on the continent.

CHAPTER EIGHT

The most devastating raid.

Up until that time in my life, my visits to the dentist had been for routine check-ups only, but for a couple of weeks I had been getting some pain in one of my back teeth, and I now faced my first 'necessary visit', which had been fixed for the early afternoon, on Tuesday May 25th. 1943.   Our dentist, Mr.Elliot, had a practice in Old Steine and had been the family dentist for quite some time.   I wasn't looking forward to this at all and it was with some trepidation that I got up that morning to start the day - but quickly put this to the back of my mind when I remembered that I had to get to school a quarter of an hour earlier than usual, to play a very important game of marbles with an arch rival of mine; each of us putting up our largest and best marble as the prize for this special match.   These attractive marbles were much larger than the ordinary ones and worth, in value, six ordinary marbles each.   I walked quickly along the Eastern Road, but was stopped by a gentleman in a light blue uniform outside the Sussex County Hospital. Recognising what school I was from by my cap, he asked me if I knew a boy called 'Enfield', - "his son" - he said; - I told him I knew him quite well and that only the other day I had had a friendly 'spar' with him in the boxing ring of the college gymnasium, under the ever watchful eye of Sgt.Major Beckett - the school gym instructor.   He told me that he had arrived at the hospital the previous night; he was apparently in the army, but undergoing hospital treatment for something - and this necessitated the uniform he was wearing, for some reason.   He asked me to take a message to his son.   I said I'd be glad to - and hurried on my way to my match which was to be played on the path beside the quadrangle in front of Bristol house. This meeting had made me a little late and I arrived to find

111

my opponent impatiently waiting at the appointed place of conflict. The match began, and a few seconds later I was minus my treasured sixer!   At disastrous moments such as these, stoicism should be shown at all costs, and so, I half-heartedly admitted that I had been beaten by the 'better man' on the day, even if he had been 'jammy' enough to hit my treasured marble from thirty feet away - with his first shot!

The lessons that morning seemed to go more quickly than usual, but my concentration wasn't particularly good as I was now somewhat preoccupied again with the thought of the dreaded dental appointment that afternoon.   At mid-day I was allowed to get ready to go home for lunch and an afternoon off school because of this appointment.   Before I left off, my form master gave me a talking to about not getting my 'prep' done correctly the night before - calling it "a poor effort" - which I suppose it was!   He told me to do it again, as well as doing another 'prep' set for that night.   I then spent a few minutes watching another 'important' marbles match, and then started on my walk home along the Eastern Road - the time was approximately 12.15pm.   I had got nearly as far as the Sussex County Hospital when everything seemed to happen at once.   First the siren went; this stopped me in my tracks and I hesitated for a few seconds - wondering whether to seek cover in the hospital - an idea which I immediately dismissed because of my fear of hospitals, or carry on and run home; about half a mile away - or run back to school, only about two hundred yards away.   Suddenly, there seemed to be explosions coming from all around me, and the sound   of aeroplanes was almost deafening; I could also hear the guns on the seafront giving off a heavy barrage.   In fact, you could say that - one minute it was nice and peaceful, and the next - all hell broke loose!   Under these circumstances, my mind was very quickly made up for me, and with 'my heart in my mouth' and extremely frightened, I ran as fast as my legs would carry me back to school, which was only a few seconds away at the pace I was going!   I

112

ran through the arch at the opening to the college on the Eastern Road, and almost ran into Mr. Burstow, the assistant head master, who was standing just by the quadrangle, outside the entrance to Bristol House; he was shading his eyes with a book which he held in one hand, and was watching a couple of German aeroplanes flying straight over the college in the direction of the sports ground - another aircraft seemed to circle the school - but then flew off in an easterly direction. We didn't see any bombs dropped by these aeroplanes, but we heard some machine-gun fire, and we both saw the pilot in the one that circled over the school. We later found out that these were Focke-Wulf 190's. Mr. Burstow, who had already grabbed me by the arm, hurried me into the school and down to the basement of Bristol House, which was used as a shelter. For several more minutes we could hear more bombs going off, some of these quite close to us, and the noise from all the Bofors guns along the seafront, was continuous and very loud. The whole air raid was very frightening for all of us, and from what I can remember, the staff and some of the older boys did a very good job in comforting several of the youngest boys, who were crying and were very distressed. Eventually, the noise stopped and there was a tense sort of silence. We stayed where we were for about another ten minutes, and then, although I can't remember hearing it, we were told that the all clear had gone and that we could all return to the assembly room on the ground floor. I didn't know quite what to do, and asked Mr.Stokes, the headmaster - telling him about my dental appointment; which at that time was obviously the least of anyone's worries; however, he went off to phone my parents, returning a few minutes later to tell me that everything was alright at home - which was a relief to me - and that I was to start walking back along the Eastern Road, where my mother would meet me halfway. What hadn't been taken into consideration was that many nearby places had been hit by the bombs, and this included some of the Eastern Road area as well as many other nearby places, so, after I had got just past the Sussex County Hospital, I found that the police and A.R.P.

wardens were blocking the Eastern Road off, I could also see that there was smoke coming from the direction of St.Marys Hall. One of the policemen asked me where I was heading for; I told him, and he said I was to go down Chesham Place, a small road just nearby, and then along Rock Street and up into the square from there. I told him about my mother meeting me, and he said that she would be told at the other end, and would probably meet me in Rock Street. There was glass lying on the road and on the pavements in Chesham Place and there were floating bits and pieces of ash and stuff in the air, and a strong smell of burning and smoke everywhere. I had noticed that Eaton Place, just nearby, had been bombed and that it was now closed by the police. The A.R.P. and an ambulance were there as well as a small crowd of onlookers. On turning into Rock Street I immediately saw my mother, and quickly told her about all that I had seen since leaving off from the college; I also told her about Eaton Place being hit; - this especially worried her as she knew some people who lived there, and this included one particularly good friend of hers, so, holding my hand, she walked me to the bottom of that road, and on getting there, she was immediately reassured, because she could see that the house where her friend lived, was undamaged and well away from the houses that had been hit. The damage at the bottom of the road looked terrible, and I can remember seeing one woman being carried on a stretcher, with another woman, with blood on her face, walking beside the stretcher, holding her hand, and muttering over and over - "God help us!" My mother, not wanting me to see any more, clutched my hand even more tightly and we turned and walked back along Rock Street - here and there avoiding walking on piles of broken glass, and even walking onto the road just in time to avoid being hit by a pane of glass - that quite simply - 'fell to the ground' as we passed by. We eventually arrived at number thirteen after stopping briefly to see smoke coming from the Arundel Road area and also that the gas works were once again on fire. Another thing we had noticed after turning up from Rock Street, was that there was a lot of activity going on near St.Mary's Hall main school on the Eastern Road, and also quite a

114

bit of smoke coming from the buildings. Amongst the rescue parties there, we saw several of the Lake Superior Regiment soldiers that we knew - they were in shirt sleeves and covered in dust - all of them looked grim and very determined.

There have been many varying reports and versions of stories about that devastating air raid, and to say which were right and which were exaggerated is very difficult. The Evening Argus on Wednesday May 26th. said that there were probably 20 F.W.190's, and that of those - four had been shot down, and that there were children among the 12 known to have died. Later it was confirmed that there were no less than 24 F.W.190's and that the death toll was 24. They also said that if it hadn't been for the R.A.F., there would have been another similar raid later that evening - it says, "An Air Ministry and Ministry of Home Communique last night stated :-

'Late last evening enemy fighter-bombers attempted to attack a town on the south east coast of England. They were intercepted by our fighters and driven off."

This seems to confirm that the mid-day raid was no sneak raid aiming at anything, as had been thought, - but a planned attack on an area that looked from the air as a likely place where invasion preparations were building up - judging by all the equipment and vehicles that could now be quite easily seen - and these included the Bren-gun carriers and tanks of the Canadian Regiments and also those of the Lake Superior Regiment in and around Sussex Square. The square itself hadn't actually been hit, but parts of the Eastern Road nearby, and also some buildings at St.Marys Hall and houses at Eaton Place and Chichester Place, were hit - with some fatalities. Arundel Road had been attacked again as had Marine Gate where there were casualties, but no fatalities. The gas works had also been hit again and this immediately resulted in the loss of a large amount of gas and left many people without the means to cook - and that included us! Many other areas in Brighton and Hove were also attacked in the ten minutes or so that this

115

carnage took place in.

In his book, IN THE FACE OF DANGER, Lt.Col.Stanley's statistics for that day are 'a bit over the top', but of course there were many varying reports at that time; and his version of what took place is not in question and I emphasise that the Lake Superiors were superb during this crisis. They took part in both trying to gun down the enemy as well as helping in the mopping up and rescue activities that took part immediately after the raid.

From chapter XI, - 'Straining at the Leash' - the following account of the raid can be found:-

"Of all the raids upon Brighton, and they were frequent enough during these mid-years of the war, one of the most serious was that which occured on May 25th. The German radio had announced several weeks previously, through the nasal, penetrating voice of William Joyce, Lord Haw Haw, the American born Irishman who had left England to join the National Socialist party, that German planes would soon make it HOT for 'Worthington's circus.' And they did. Shortly after the noon hour had sounded, some twenty fighter-bombers, FW's 190, struck at Brighton. The vehicles of the Lake Superiors, Bren-gun carriers, trucks, cars, motorcycles, were parked in the streets and in the parking areas and there was no time to move them to shelter. For about ten minurtes the German planes flew up and down, bombing and machine - gunning as they went.

The area immediately adjacent battalion headquarters was badly jarred and the building adjoining St.Mary's Hall was damaged by a falling bomb. Headquarters company at Arundel place was also mauled by cannon and machine gun fire.

The men were at lunch when the raiders arrived, but no sooner did the planes depart than they went into action. The local A.R.P. took some time to get organized, and it was a group of Lake Superiors under Sgt.C.J.Barnes who first began to dig the victims out of the ruins and the rubble. So feverishly did they work, that, at St.Mary's Hall, they managed to extract three casualties from the pile of jagged brick, crumbling plaster and broken glass, before the

A.R.P. men had arrived on the scene.

Similar incidents took place in other parts of Brighton as the officers took hold of the situation and organized rescue squads.

The work continued throughout the afternoon and well into the night. The following day a party under Captain Mackenzie was still digging. They unearthed an old man, 79 years of age, but still 'alive, and swearing a blue streak.' The civilian casualties were numerous, estimates of those killed running as high as two hundred. Fortunately, only fourteen Canadians lost their lives and of these none were members of the Lake Superior Regiment.   Neither soldiers nor civilians would readily forget the raid of May 25th., and the people of Brighton gratefully expressed their thanks for the help and friendly sympathy given them by the Canadian soldiers in their midst."

When Col.Stanley was commissioned to write 'In The Face of Danger', - it was in the 1950's - not many years after the end of the war, so, obtaining the actual statistics at that time, might have been more difficult - but two hundred dead just wasn't the case, and the official list of twenty four 'civilians' dead, gives the names and addresses and is corroborated. As for the fourteen dead Canadian soldiers; they must be on some military list, but I can find no mention of this anywhere. The rest of the account though, I believe is accurate, and it makes sense.

As far as the rescue work is concerned, including searching for people buried under rubble and clearing up after the raid - I actually witnessed some of this, and also remember the bits and pieces I was told by my parents. I know that my father had a very high regard for the A.R.P. and had friends and acquaintances who were members of it - he always said that they did "a hell of a good job", and I remember that everyone was praised for their rescue work - British and Canadians alike. Concerning the damage at St.Marys' Hall; back in the July of 1941, almost exactly a year after they had been closed down for the duration, the governors of the school declared their intention to re-open after the war, but the bomb that had fallen on

117

the main school on the Eastern Road, had hit some terraced houses converted for school use, and this had some more far reaching consequences for the school.   I quote a short passage which can be found on page 33 of 'A short History of St.Marys Hall 1836-1992.'

'Fate was to take a final hand in order to make the re-opening more difficult for on the 25th May 1943 a bomb fell on Hervey Terrace destroying the lodge, 227 and 229 Eastern Road and badly damaging the laboratory. This bomb may have been a blessing in disguise in the long term, for the old houses were quite unsuitable to form part of the school that was to arise when peace was finally restored. After the war it was decided to build 'Elliot House' to accommodate some sixty boarders on the site of the bombed houses in Hervey Terrace. By September 1951 the house was ready, and to start with occupied by twenty- two boarders. The old science laboratory that had also been damaged in the raid had been converted for use as a domestic science room and also came into use that September.'

Of the German aircraft; the most likely account is that two separate waves of F.Ws 190 came to attack the town, one wave coming in from an Easterly direction and flying low near the cliffs between Rottingdean and Black Rock before making their attack on the Kemptown area, and the second slightly larger wave coming in from the sea close to the Palace Pier, and then for ten minutes or so, circling around the towns - bombing and machine gunning various places as they did so.

Early that evening most of our crowd met in the top gardens. "It all happened so quickly". I said - I had been telling them what happened to me when the raid started.

"My sister said my mother knows someone who got killed at Eaton Place." Timmy said.

"My mother knows someone there,- but she was alright." I said. It was at this point that we saw Cyril come into the gardens - we called out to him to come and join us, but he wouldn't. He stood near the bottom of the tree for a while, and, amongst other things told us that one of

118

his relatives had been injured in the raid and that a friend of his mother's had been killed. He looked very gloomy and soon walked off; we felt sorry for him.

Janine, sitting on the branch immediately below me, said, "just look at the sea now, it all looks so calm and peaceful, isn't it horrible to think that at any moment we might see aeroplanes coming from the horizon, which within seconds could be dropping bombs on us and killing us!" We spent another half hour in the gardens and then made our different ways home.

That evening my parents had a local walkabout, seeing some of the damage done in our immediate area of Kemptown. They walked round to the Clyde Arms at Bristol Gardens for a drink and a chat with some of the locals, this pub, for some reason, was nicknamed 'The Hogswallopers', and is just behind the square. They saw the damage done at Princes Terrace and Bennett Road and talked to some of the residents they recognised. They were distressed to learn that someone they knew slightly who lived in Bennett Road had been killed. They ventured to several other places and saw further damage there, but had kept clear of the gas works area as there was still plenty of activity going on there - including the fire brigade still being 'hard at it!' Eventually, feeling very depressed, they returned home and told us of all they'd seen.

In the years to come there were times when I had nightmares about that raid, and would sometimes wake up in the night, screaming out. It was always about the same incident during the raid - when I had run into the school and bumped into Mr.Burstow as the enemy planes circled above us, - the difference being that in the nightmare, the cockpit of one of the planes opens up and a German, with a horrible sneer on his face, leans out of the aeroplane holding a bomb in his hands and chucks it down at us, -- at that point I would wake up!

The next day we learned of the enemy activity in other parts of the towns, and all manner of horrific reports came to our ears. Someone we knew who worked at The Sussex County hospital told of the pandemonium and 'blood, sweat and tears' throughout the day immediately after the raid.

The four of us met up again the next evening, this time in the bottom gardens at the horseshoe, where the main topic once again was about the day before, with each of us telling of more happenings during and after the raid, that we had learned about that day - during which some of the rescue work had still been going on. The subject soon changed however when I produced a large slab of very hard toffee which had been given to me by one of the Canadian soldiers, just as I was leaving the house. He had told me to share it with my friends. It was so hard we couldn't break it by hand, so I banged it hard on the low stone wall on the inside of the horseshoe - it was very brittle, and broke up into scores of pieces, and we spent the next several minutes trying to share them all out equally. After quite a bit of haggling, we eventually arrived at what we considered to be four equal portions - and sitting on the seats we commenced our feast. Unfortunately the action of banging the toffee bar against the wall of the horseshoe had disturbed some bees, who were now appearing from a small hole in the stonework, and flying angrily all around us. When we considered it safe to return to our seats, we carried on chewing at the toffee, and almost immediately, I felt a sudden sharp pain on my right ear. I jumped up from the seat, yelling out at the same time, on the top of my voice - "I've been stung!" The bee, that had now gasped it's last breath, fell to the ground, and on seeing this, which confirmed that I had indeed been stung by a bee, I started a noisy war dance, telling everyone of the pain that I was in and hoping that this peculiar activity might sooth it. A lady that we knew slightly, who'd been sitting just outside the horseshoe, came over and told me to stand still, and with a pair of tweezers she had taken from her handbag, proceeded to extract the sting, whilst I, weak at the knees, tried to put on a brave face. With the sting removed, the lady insisted on walking me back to my home and making sure my mother knew all about it. On arriving back at number thirteen my mother wondered whether I needed medical attention, and was in two minds about this, but although the ear had swollen and had gone extremely red, the pain didn't seem too bad now, and I said so, in the hope that I could return to the gardens again - but this was not to be, and I spent the rest of the day 'under observation' indoors, and that determined me to keep well clear of angry bees in the future. 'Honey,' I felt was very nice, but its manufacturers - something to be wary of! A bit later I overheard my mother telling a friend on the phone, "-- he gets caught out during the beginning of that ghastly raid without any harm coming to him - and then goes out and gets stung by a bee!"

On the Friday of that week Mr.Campbell made one of his fortnightly visits to my father for a 'healing' session, and after that he told my parents - with me having just arrived home from school for lunch and listening in - about his "awful day", on the day of the big raid. He had been visiting another one of his 'patients' at St.Lukes Terrace - not far from Queens Park, and also not far from a road called 'Downs Terrace', which none of us had ever heard of before. Apparently this little terraced road had been badly hit during the raid, with many injured and at least six fatalities. He told us how he had hurried to the scene just minutes after the all clear, and had been one of many who had tried to help. Some shops had been hit there, burying several people, still alive, under the rubble - and he and some other ordinary civilians had helped the fire brigade and A.R.P.who were professionally getting on with the rescue work - whilst instructing the likes of Mr.Campbell, where they could be most useful.
Mr.Campbell's visit ended on a happier note as he told me another story of the North American Indians and their ways of life. On another day he would tell me the tragic story of 'Wounded Knee', carefully portraying as vivid a picture as he thought was necessary for someone of my age, but as he said, "we've had enough of gloom and doom for today!" Instead, he told me how the Indians used to 'count coup ', to show their bravery and resolve some of their arguments - by trying to get something over on their enemies. After he'd gone, my father, who'd been listening as well, said, "what a pity that the differences between the warring nations of today couldn't be resolved in such non-violent ways!"

121

At the week-end, on a fine Sunday morning at the end of that eventful month of May, my mother and I walked over the downs to Ovingdean; "For a bit of peace and serenity - and also for soothing my nerves!" - she said. Whilst walking, we played a familiar game for us on walks such as this, - a sort of 'eye spy', with the aim being to spot as many birds, insects and animals as possible as we went on our way. Amongst the many creatures we saw that day, were a kestrel hovering quite close to us, a weasel quickly dashing from one side of the path in front of us to the long grass and safety of the other side - some horses in a fenced off small field; cows grazing in a meadow - not too far away, and some rabbits scampering about in the grass by some low stone walls, built around a small pasture - just near St.Wulfran's church, which nestled tranquilly below a picturesque sweep of the downs. For a little while the war had gone out of our minds and the beauty of these surroundings soothed stretched nerves and gave my mother, just for a while, the peace of mind she was seeking. We attended the service with not more than a couple of dozen other people. On our way back over the downs my mother talked of her love of the countryside - especially of Ovingdean, and she said to me, "one day I'd like to live here -- would you?" I replied, that I would - "very much indeed", and could imagine adventurous times on the wide open spaces of the Sussex Downs; but what I didn't say to her was that I would also miss the gardens and my friends at Sussex Square, which of course meant a great deal to me. She carried on talking about the village and also said, "it'd be a nice place to rest my weary bones when my time comes!" I squeezed her hand a bit more tightly when she said this - she laughed, and looking closely at me, said, "it's alright, there's plenty more living to do yet!"

During the next two years we were to make this walk quite a few more times together, and the paths we walked then, are still there today, and although some of the landscape has changed - the beauty remains.

CHAPTER NINE

A bet on the Derby. – Empty houses.

Private Charles Gordon, of the 1st. Airborne Division, arrived at number thirteen at the beginning of June 1943. My 'new' Uncle Charles had got a few days leave to be with his wife and baby son and had arrived in a borrowed car with a full tank of petrol and coupons enough to do plenty of driving about during those few days respite from military duties. Although his first priorities were for Daphne and Charles junior, he said he was determined to go to the Derby at Newmarket the next day, now that he had the use of the car, and asked who wanted to go with him. Daphne said that she certainly wouldn't take the baby all that distance; my mother said that she would sooner stay with Daphne; Jill, who wasn't there at the time, but was asked later, said that she had other arrangements - and I said that I'd love to go, but was quickly told that I had a backlog of homework to do and that that came first; so that put paid to my chances; but my father, as the idea grew on him; despite the probable discomfort of sitting in a car for so long with his false leg, said he'd very much like to see this Derby, which was now being run at Newmarket instead of Epsom, as were all the wartime Derby meetings. The next day, before they went, I was shown the paper and told to pick out the horse of my choice for the big race, and was told that there would be a shilling each way riding on it for me - Jill got the same offer. Daphne and my mother had slightly larger wagers than us - two and sixpence each way each on their selections. My father and Uncle Charles were going there hoping to see Gordon Richards, the champion jockey, win his first Derby on 'Nasrullah', something of an outsider; however they both said they'd have a saver on the favourite as well. Mother picked a horse called 'Umidadd' for her two and sixpence each way, partly because she liked the name and partly "women's intuition," she said.   I can't remember what Jill or my aunt backed, but I picked a horse called 'Straight Deal' for my bob each way - I can't remember why, but I do know that that was my first bet ever.

That evening, my father and Uncle Charles arrived home after spending an hour drowning their sorrows at the Rock Inn. They had both lost not only on the Derby but also on all the other races. Daphne and Jill had also lost; - my mothers horse though had come second at the good price of 100/8 - so she'd made a profit on the race - - but I 'd backed the winner - 'Straight Deal', which had duly obliged at 100/6, and after my father had taken the weight off his feet he took a crisp one pound note from his wallet and - just a little begrudgingly - handed it to me. I was now nearly a millionaire and determined to stay so - well that is until the shops opened!

A couple of days later we were sitting on the lower branches of our tree, just idling away the time. "What sort of sweet are you sucking?" Peter asked me - rather obviously hoping I might give him one; he knew only too well though, that when we had run out of our sweet coupons, which entitled us to just eight ounces of sweets a month, that we sometimes bought cough sweets - such as Zubes or Victory V lozenges - as they didn't require coupons.

"It's an 'iodized throat tablet'" I said "they're all I could get."
I had bought them from 'Hewitts' the chemists in St.Georges Road on my way home from school, making the detour purposefully in the quest for some sweets that I could buy without coupons from some of my winnings. I handed them round. Barry Power was the first to spit his out, then, surprisingly, Peter did the same. Barry's sister, Jill, politely took her's from her mouth and said - "it tastes horrid!"   I now found myself in the amazing predicament of being in possession of some 'sweets' that were actually going to last! That was until my father saw me with them, and thinking that they looked as if they could be harmful to me - promptly confiscated them!   "Zubes, and things like that, I suppose, are not too bad," he said, "but even then only in moderation; these though, look quite

dangerous and I'm surprised the chemist sold them to you!" -- with that he put the offending lozenges in a small drawer in his desk - and that, I thought, was the end of the matter; but that evening I noticed he was sucking something, and said - "dad are you sucking one of my throat tablets?" - He made some sort of affirmative answer to this by mumbling something like, "a bit of a smokers cough," and I decided not to pursue the matter any further. I also thought better of asking him for a part refund on my outlay for them!

The next day I bought some yellow coloured bits of stick-like stuff from the sweet shop in Sudely Place - next to the old 'Kings-cliff' cinema - these also required no coupons, and were called 'Liquorice root.' My father on seeing me chewing away at this - didn't confiscate it, but said to my mother - "my God - the boy not only climbs trees - now he eats them!"

In early August, when the summer once again reminded us of long hot days spent on the beach before the war, Jill and I remembered our mothers promise of taking us for a picnic and a swim at a spot on the river Adur, where it flowed not far from the lower sports fields of Lancing College. We had been told of a particularly nice place, just near the river bank, by our friends, 'the Whitehead's', who lived at South Lancing. They had suggested to my mother that it would be nice if we could all meet there for a picnic one day. Mother kept her promise, and on a fine, very warm day, shortly after breaking up for the summer holidays, we caught the Southdown bus from Poole Valley - which took us through Shoreham and over the toll bridge which spans the Adur, and then got off at the stop by the Sussex Pad Hotel, and started on the walk - of between a half and three quarters of a mile - along a tree lined country road to our designated picnic place. The road we walked was the one that goes from the Sussex Pad at North Lancing to the small market town of Steyning, which lies picturesquly below the south downs at the foot of the steep and legendary Chanctonbury

125

Ring. We were soon settled in the right place, and half an hour later Edie Whitehead and her husband Harold arrived with their son Peter and a friend of his. We had over an hour's wait before the high tide, when it would not only be safer to swim, but also not so muddy, as you didn't have so far from the river bank to the water. As this was our first visit to this place, my mother felt she didn't want the responsibility of taking some of my friends with us until she knew more about the lay of the land and the ways of the river. Jill, being that much older, brought some friends of her own age, including her new boyfriend, Alec Peak, and two boys we knew well from the square - David Turrel and Tony Morton. All of us were good swimmers, but when we did eventually get into the bracing salt water, we heeded the advice, "not to try to swim out to the middle of the river, and to be careful of the currents." These currents however, weren't running too strongly just for a while, now that the tide was fully high. As the day wore on, the banks of the river became more and more crowded, and by shortly after 2pm, it looked more like Brighton beach near the Palace Pier on a hot August bank holiday!

During that day, Edie Whitehead told my mother that the pupils and staff at Lancing College had been evacuated to Shropshire during 1940, and H.M.S. King Alfred officers training school, were in residence there at the moment; but it would revert back to normal at the end of the war, and she hoped to send Peter there when this happened. Mother told her that she also had designs on sending me to Lancing; but in those days that was just a distant dream, and little could she have dreamt that day, that in slightly less than five years time, during the summer term of 1948, I would be in my second year at this famous public school - during it's centenary celebrations - when we would quite often see Benjamin Britten, an old boy of the school, in the company of his friend and associate, Peter Pears, while they were writing and presenting the music for this special occasion.

By just after four o'clock and with the tide well on the ebb, we decided to pack all the picnic things up and get ready for the journey home. I noticed that there were still quite a few people in the water, and those that we watched making their way back to the grass by the river bank, and wherever they'd left their clothes, were all muddy from the ankles down and would find it difficult to get it cleaned off unless they'd brought something with them to wash it off with - that was why we'd chosen to swim on the high tide when the water was nearly up to the top of the river bank. By the time we left off, there were still so many people standing in and around the river and in the fields close to it, that on reflecting on that scene in later life - it conjures up in my mind a biblical scene, with John the Baptist being the one person missing from it. We said good-bye to our friends after promising to meet again at the same place two weeks later, when the tides would be right once again, and hopefully, the weather as well. During those holidays we had two more enjoyable visits to the river.

For the residents of Sussex Square and some other nearby areas, something happened during the first half of that month that both surprised and saddened us. On Thursday August 12th. we awoke to a strange sort of silence - something was missing. We soon realized that there weren't the usual sounds of the 'hustle and bustle' of army life going on outside. On looking out of the window my mother saw that all the vehicles of the Lake Superior Regiment had gone; she walked a few yards up the square and could see that St.Nicholas House was now completely empty. A little later we discovered that the whole regiment had departed in the early hours. All the places that they had occupied, including the main buildings of St.Mary's Hall on the Eastern Road, now stood deserted and sadly empty of everything. There had been no warning - no goodbyes - nothing! They had, quite simply, with no noise or palaver, uprooted and gone. After the war, we found out that this was the way their senior command had ordered it; in other words, the less said about their movements, the better! It wasn't long

127

however before we found out that thay had only moved along the coast a few miles to Worthing, so, just for a while, important contacts could still be made, including further meetings between the more serious of the courting couples. Within a month though even this close link was severed when the regiment moved once again - this time, as Lt./Col. Stanley describes it - to "The Brecklands of Norfolk."

That part of our lives, shared with these men, was now over; for most of us - it was sad - but of course it was also war! On the morning it was discovered that they had gone from the square - at first there was much speculation; the most popular theory being that the invasion of the continent was imminent - but on finding out just where thay had gone to after leaving Worthing, this idea, though not discounted, was temporarily put to the back of our minds.

A few days later we had another bad air raid. This time I was woken up in the night to go down to the basement to shelter - something that hadn't happened for quite a while. The raid took place in the very early hours of the 16th. August. Although we heard plenty of explosions and gun-fire from nearby, the square once more went unscathed, and apart from various accounts of what had been hit from some of the people my parents talked to that day - in the Evening Argus a report of the raid says:-

'Six enemy aircraft were destroyed in raids on the south east coast of England last night. Bombs were dropped on a place on the south coast of England causing damage and casualties, including a number of people killed.' What we had found out for ourselves, was that the bombs had been dropped near and around Wilson's Avenue; this is the road that leads from the south westerly corner of East Brighton Park, goes up over the downs, and crosses Brighton racecourse by the five furlong gate, before meeting the road that leads from the town to Woodingdean. Several places were hit, including, in Whitehawk, where an air raid warden was one of the fatalities.'

128

On August 17th. the news from abroad was that Sicily had been taken by the allies, and on September 3rd, exactly four years after the war had been declared in England - Italy was invaded and surrendered. The Germans had other ideas though, and on September 10th, they seized Rome, thus making 'The Eternal City', German occupied territory.

In mid September, we had our usual blackberrying expedition; this time rather a wet one, as there were frequent thundery showers. We picked until my mother said we had "an adequate amount". Just before making our way back home again we were thrilled to see a fox disappearing into the bracken - over the years we had aways hoped to see one, and this was our first sighting. Apart from this harvest of blackberries, and the few vegetables we grew on a small 'shared' allotment, not far from the back of St.Marks church, the bottom gardens, that year, provided us with another - most unexpected crop. Where the grass had been allowed to grow longer, beyond the barbed wire, we were surprised to see that there were some large mushrooms growing at one particular place, near a small clump of trees on the easterly side of the gardens - either none of the soldiers who could use that side of the wire had seen them - or they just weren't interested in picking them. I told my parents about this and they came and had a look for themselves. Father remarked, "they look like horse mushrooms and would make a tasty meal, a pity we can't get to them!" A little later, after they had gone home, I squeezed my agile slim body through the barbed wire, taking good care not to get caught up on it, and quickly picked what I thought would be enough for a couple of meals for us, then, placing them half-way through the wire, I carefully made my way back to our part of the gardens. I put all the mushrooms in my jacket, and picking up my bundle of spoils, I quickly made my way home - I was feeling very pleased with myself and was expecting something of a hero's welcome when I got there! It came as a bit of a shock therefore when both my parents angrily told me that if there had been mines there, I could have been blown up! I said that we all knew there weren't any mines there, because we'd seen soldiers walking all over the area; to which they said that - "in any case it was out of bounds as I very well knew and that I had blatantly disobeyed their orders never to try to get through the barbed wire." After a while they relented a bit, and the flat was soon filled with the smell of frying bacon, mushrooms, and tomatoes. I ate the portion that had been given to me, but didn't like them all that much, and thought the whole operation was something of a failure; however, it was not to be the last time I would cross the wire.

With the departure of most of the Canadians and various other military units from the Brighton area, the war seemed a bit quieter now on the homefront; also, the Luftwaffe, apart from one or two 'sneak raids', hadn't unleashed any further devastating attacks on us - such as the big air raids in May and August. My father said that it was rather like being 'in limbo' and remarked that everyone that he had talked to, were all wondering when the invasion of France would take place. With all the troop movements of Americans,Canadians and others, not to mention our own forces, it was felt that this, so obviously planned for attack, was overdue. These, however, were the feelings of the laymen - the 'Brass Hats' were the decision makers and the elements - 'The Divine Hand of Providence' - in other words the weather would obviously play a very important part in crossing the channel. With the onset of another wartime winter, it was no cheer to anyone that the hoped for assault would now almost certainly not be until the spring at the earliest.

On December 1st. my father received the news that his favourite uncle, the cricketing one, who was also called Lance, and who lived at Ditchling, had died after a short illness. I had been told many stories about this, 'quite famous', great uncle of mine, who I had also met on several memorable occasions. A very

130

popular character, he had been christened, - 'William Lancelot Knowles,' - but was nearly always called 'Lance' by his friends and associates - why the William was usually dropped - I have no idea. He had played cricket for Kent and Sussex and had also been secretary of Sussex C.C.C.. He was an 'amateur' player.

In a letter from Mr.C.H.Taylor, the curator for Kent C.C.C. - he says that my great uncle played in 34 matches for Kent, including, in a match at the Oval against Surrey in 1900, scoring 124, and with J.R.Mason, put on 248 for the fourth wicket in 160 minutes. In some more correspondence about him from Robert Boddie, librarian for Sussex C.C.C. - Mr.Boddie says that W.L.Knowles was secretary for the club from 1922 until just before his death in 1943. He played just once for Sussex. He also played for the 'Sussex Gentlemen', and for some years was 'Master of Brighton Foot Beagles.' He was also a J.P. In a book by the well known cricketer, A.E.R.Gilligan, called, 'Sussex Cricket', the following passage appears:- '--Luckily in 1921 Sussex was fortunate enough to secure, on the retirement of Major W.G.M.Sarel, who had done a great deal for cricket since the war, one of our vice-presidents, Mr.W.L.Knowles, J.P., to take on the secretaryship of the club. What Sussex now owes to Lance Knowles would take more than my pen would adequately describe!' I remember my father telling me stories of him alongside the names of many famous cricketers, including Maurice Tate, Jack Hobbs, Duleep, George Cox and Jim Langridge. I can remember him from the visits he, and Aunt May, made to us, and from the journeys we now and again made to Ditchling, where they lived. The thing I remember the most about him on those visits, was that just as we were about to leave each time, he would secretively press a half-crown piece into my hand, and while doing so, put his finger to his mouth - telling me that the transaction was strictly just between him and me! Both my mother and father attended the funeral, and over the years to come, the stories about him continued and never failed to entertain.

On breaking up from school for the Christmas holidays, my sister told me that she was in two minds about going carol singing again that year and that it would probably be better to make some other plans of my own. I asked my mother whether I could form a small group from my own friends, and she said that she had no objections as long as we kept to the square and the crescents. I then asked Janine, Peter, Michael, and Brenda Barrett to join me, and they agreed. I also asked Jill and Barry Power, but they couldn't come. Timmy, after thinking about it for a while, also declined to join us. Cyril, who had turned up in the top gardens on the first day of the holidays, on hearing us talking about it, asked to join us on the Christmas eve, and we agreed, hoping we hadn't let ourselves in for anything we might regret! The remaining days before Christmas we spent in a flurry of activity getting everything organised for the big night, and this included, on my insistence, making sure that we all knew the words to at least six carols; so we did some practice singing in the gardens, sometimes even while we were sitting near the top of 'our tree' - thereby giving quite a few of the people we would call on, on the night - a preview. The big day quickly arrived, and at half past six precisely, we excitedly began our evening of carol singing to some of the residents nearby; most of whom we knew slightly - but also a few that we didn't. It was a cold dry evening with a light northerly wind and just the odd patches of cloud in an otherwise bright and starry sky. Cyril joined us just as we were starting off; saying that his mother had given him such a large meal - "to stoke him up for the evening ahead" - that he had got stomach ache and nearly hadn't made it! At one of the first flats we called on, the occupant, a writer we knew slightly, asked us in and gave us a piece of fruit cake each as well as some loose change; I held on to my piece of cake instead of eating it there and then like the others did, because I couldn't and still can't, eat raisins,sultanas or any other form of dried friut, apart from in Christmas pudding form - so, when the gentleman's back was turned, I put it into my coat pocket. A few calls later, a lady, who we also knew slightly, gave us each a handful of nuts and raisins - so I carefully selected the nuts to eat and put the raisins in the same pocket as the piece of cake. At another place where we were specially asked to sing as an encore - 'Once in Royal Davids City' - we were given two half-crown pieces, a glass of lemonade and a mince pie each; my mince pie joined the fruit cake and raisins in my coat pocket. At another flat we were each given a 'pomegranate' and a 'medlar' by the occupant, a senior ranking serviceman who had just returned home from overseas. The medlar was "nice and soft and rotten and just as they were supposed to be eaten!" he told us; - this time I noticed that the others also made excuses and said that they'd eat them later, and my ones of course went into the same pocket as the cake, the raisins and the mince pie, making it something of a 'storage larder'! At another house, this time in Lewes Crescent and only a couple of houses from where Peter lived, we were standing in the hallway outside a flat where an elderly couple lived, and were singing 'The Holly and the Ivy', - we had just got to the part of the chorus which goes " - The playing of the merry organ, sweet singing in the choir." - When Cyril, very loudly, broke wind. At embarrassing moments like these, it's very difficult to know what it's best to do; -- in other words do you say, "pardon me" - and leave it at that, - do you carry on as though nothing has happened, - do you openly reprimand the offending culprit, or do you, as we did, - become overcome by the whole thing, and spontaneously all break out into fits of giggles. The elderly couple looked at us in some amazement, and it suddenly occurred to me that perhaps they hadn't even heard the offending sound and couldn't make out what we were laughing about. Apologising to them, and telling them that something particularly funny had happened just before we had entered the house and we still couldn't stop laughing about it, we then made our escape down the wide staircase and out onto the pavement for some much needed fresh air - where, with a few choice remarks to Cyril - and still giggling - we continued to on to a few more houses before calling it an evening. We shared the money out in our living room and decided that half of the total would go to six of the old men at the workhouse; these six included Kingy, Frank and Dopey and three others we had come to know and like. Instead of giving them cash we would give them tobacco, cigarettes, and for Dopey - some chocolate; I was also pretty sure that my parents would add their own contribution to this. We didn't say anything to them about the incident with Cyril of course, and after a hot drink we said our goodnights. Before going to bed my mother asked me what the bulge was in my coat pocket; after I had hesitated in answering her, she decided to look for herself, and what she pulled out of it could only be described as a horrible mess. At first, she wasn't at all amused, but she quickly saw the funny side of it, and the only other remark she made about it, was to say - "what a waste!" For all of us it had been an enjoyable evening and something to remember. We agreed to do the same thing again next year - secretly though I had a feeling that Cyril might not get another invitation - but a year was a long time away!

Our Christmas pillow cases that year contained a little more in the way of sweets; this was because our monthly ration for these had gone up from eight ounces to twelve ounces, with the E coupons increasing from one ounce each to two ounces and the D's remaining at one ounce. Our selection of glass decorations were now very much depleted through breakage, and finding replacements at that time was difficult, but some homemade additions, made from various colourful materials, helped to retain the brightness and beauty of this comforting and enjoyable part of the festive season. The day was once again spent visiting friends and being visited by them. Later the Christmas tree candles were lit and before long, after an evening filled enjoyably with energetic games, it was time for bed.

The pantomine at the Hippodrome that year, 'Jack and the Beanstalk' didn't boast a big name and I remember being disappointed that 'Jill Manners' hadn't come to Brighton to star again; I still thought of her as 'very special' - but kept such thoughts strictly to myself - remembering the mild ridicule I had had to endure from friends the previous year, when it was found out that I had a crush on her.

One day shortly after Christmas, Timmy, Peter and I were allowed to go to the Odeon Kemptown cinema without being accompanied by any of our parents. Although we didn't think all that much of the main film, which had Deanna Durbin in it, the second feature, starring Chester Morris and called, 'High Explosive', was much more to our taste; but the most memorable part of that film show didn't have anything to do with what was being shown on the screen. We always made a point of sitting in the back row upstairs - if there were any of those seats available - as there were on that afternoon. Before long the cinema filled up, and sitting in the seats just in front of us were some ladies, who were all wearing hats. Despite some loud and pointed remarks from us; because we couldn't see the screen properly, they resolutely kept their hats on - one of them even turning round to us and telling us not to be so cheeky! Just before the end of the complete performance, Timmy, who had taken to secretly smoking a cigarette now and again, decided to smoke one in the darkness of the cinema. We looked across at him as he 'lit up,' and then carried on watching the climax of the film. Just before leaving the cinema, after the lights had come on, I noticed that the hat on the lady sitting in front of Timmy - the one who'd told us not to be cheeky - had smoke coming from it. Timmy had put his still lighted cigarette end in the brim of the hat - and, grinning widely - urged us to get a move on and get out of the cinema as quickly as possible. I remember that just as we were about to make our 'escape' through the door, I looked back and saw the woman still talking away to her friends completely oblivious of the fact that she was on fire - I was tempted for a moment to linger and see what happened but thought better of it and quickly joined the others on the street. I often wonder what did happen.

135

The ice rink at the bottom of West Street had now become another venue that Jill and I went to quite a lot. Jill took to the ice quite readily, but it took me quite a bit longer to learn the art of being able to keep standing up; at first I was stumbling about and falling all over the place, when not holding grimly on to the barrier. This only cost a shilling each for children, and if we didn't have our own skates - which at first we didn't - it was just another sixpence for the hire of them; however, as our parents encouraged us in this form of sporting entertainment, they usually always paid all the necessary expenses, and Saturday mornings at the rink, properly called the sports stadium, became a regular thing.

The new year arrived quietly for us, and on a mild morning in January, just a few days before the start of the new term, a small group of us walked over the bleak downs, to the spinney where we went blackberrying every summer. Since sighting the fox at our last visit there we thought it would be a good idea to explore the area in winter and see what might be there. We walked much more quickly than when we were with the adults, and chatted away as we walked. "Do you remember the pet cemetery in the wilderness?" Janine asked us in general, as we manoeuvred in single file along one of the narrow paths cut into the side of the downs - she was referring to a dense area of bushes and shrubbery that adjoined the western side of the slopes, below the bottom gardens. Someone had called it a wilderness at some time and the name had stuck. Amongst this profusion of shrubbery and bushes, a pet cemetery had been established, but when, and by whom, I have no idea; I simply remember seeing the grave stones there, and reading the rather sad words of love engraved upon them.

"I sometimes went there with my mother and Jill," I said - "why do you ask?"
"Because," Janine replied, "someone told my mother that one of the soldiers who is still allowed to go to somewhere near to there, said that not only had foxes been seen there - and on the beaches - but also polecats."

"What are polecats?" Peter asked.

"They're like ferrets," I replied, I knew this because 'Blanche', the dwarf-like little man who did odd jobs for us, kept some of them in some large hutches which he had in the small garden of his house, and on a couple of occasions he had taken me to see them.

"What are ferrets?" Peter asked.

"They're like large stoats," Janine said, "and if you ask me what stoats are - I'll scream!"

Peter kept quiet, but I said "you sound just like Violet Elizabeth Bott!" - and immediately wished I hadn't. "Ha, ha." Janine made a rude face at me, but didn't say anything else.

The blackberry patch looked very different in winter and although we glimpsed a couple of rabbits and saw plenty of pigeons flying about, there was nothing much else of any interest for us to see. After exploring by some fox holes, dug into a steepish part of the downs nearby, we began the journey home. We passed by the golf course again, and it was the first time I had ever seen it without a single player in sight. I was just about to remark on this to the others when something on a green, that was a bit less than a hundred yards away to my right, caught my eye. At first I thought it was a medium sized dog. "Look over there," I pointed to where the animal was, "I think it's a fox." I said. The others all looked. "It is a fox!" Janine said excitedly.

"Yes it definitely is." Michael said. We stood there quietly watching it for a while; it was sitting right in the middle of the green and now and again moved its head very slightly; then it looked in our direction - slowly stood up - shook itself, and then turned and lazily trotted off over the downs - its brush slowly swaying from side to side, was the last we saw of it. It had been an enjoyable experience for all of us, and certainly something very special to me.

The old men at the workhouse, who over the years had become completely settled in their pleasant and certainly very different surroundings, now, almost to a man, seemed very happy with their lot, and Frank, the quiet, well educated one, told my father that just about everyone there didn't mind in the slightest if the war carried on for ever; they liked the area - they liked the house - they liked the top gardens and they also liked most of the people; "also," Frank added laughingly – "they even liked some of the children!" He went on to say that, like many of his fellow 'inmates', he dreaded having to move back up to the race-hill and the wing of the Brighton General Hospital that had been their home before the war. There were now several new faces among these men. One of the new arrivals was a little Yorkshireman who used to suck at a pipe that had no tobacco in it and was usually upside down; whether this was a broad hint that he wouldn't say no if anybody bought him some tobacco, we couldn't guess. He had a round, permanently smiling face and we called him - 'Ee-Ba-Goom,' this was because every time you told him something, he'd think for a while - and then, before saying anything else, would say, 'Ee-Ba-Goom!' Another one who used to smell quite strongly of the beer he seemed to be able to afford to drink all the time - we called 'Wallace Beery' - after the famous film star of that era. One other one that I can remember, who was also fond of an everyday tipple, would quite often arrive back in the square from wherever he'd been, somewhat the worse for wear, and would often be seen holding tightly onto the railings of the closest basement to him, when he felt he needed support - we called him, 'Gripper'! Most of the men though had been there from the beginning, and 'Dopey' was still a familiar sight, as was 'Kingy', who still had his amazing pipe.

With the start of the new school term, the new year was well on its way; another year that would take an important place in the history books, and certainly for me, a period of my life never to be forgotten.

CHAPTER TEN

Another terror raid. – The Doodlebugs go by.

The first days back at school in the January of 1944 seemed to go very slowly. The Sweet Caporal craze, with the departure of the Canadians, was now losing some of its earlier momentum, but the collecting 'bug' had been awoken in some of us, and pre-war cigarette cards now became highly sought after, with both myself and Peter becoming enthusiasts. I also started a stamp collection, but at first I was only interested in the eye catching picturesque ones from countries like Liberia, where, instead of 'boring' figureheads on the stamps, they had brightly coloured pictures of animals in their natural environments.

My father, a keen collector himself, particularly encouraged me in this hobby. Since childhood, he had put together a very good collection of Dutch and Dutch East Indies stamps, mainly because he had very strong Dutch connections. He was born of an English father and Dutch mother; he had one brother, 'Bertie'. Hartley Knowles, his father, and the brother of the cricketing uncle, was a gold prospecting engineer and something of an adventurer; he had sunk a large chunk of family money, including borrowing money from various relatives, on an ill-fated treasure seeking adventure to South America, to try to find precious stones and gold that had once belonged to the Inca civilization. This expedition, and Hartley, are mentioned in various books about people who have tried, unsuccessfully, to find these long lost treasures.

Hartley had married Mary Vickers, the daughter of a Batavian judge, and my father was born in 1891 at the family home - 'Twineham Grange' - at the villages of Wineham and Twineham, in the heart of the Suusex countryside, near Henfield. When my father was just nine years old, Hartley and his wife agreed to separate, and the agreement was that my father would be brought

139

up by Hartley's side of the family as an English boy, and Bertie, brought up as a Dutch boy. This caused much sadness for both the boys, but this is what had happened, and they both went their seperate ways in life from then on. Mary Vickers, our 'Bournemouth grandma,' never remarried, and with Bertie carving out a life for himself in the far east and Australia, she eventually came back to live in that pleasant resort in the south of England. We used to see her on summer holidays we spent in a cottage called 'Kip- Kot' - just near where she lived and close to the sea. I remember some of the visits that we made there quite clearly and also remember, on the rainy days, watching my father as he added stamps to various albums.

By now the air raid activity in the Brighton area had quietened down considerably, but just after I had gone to sleep on one particularly cold February evening, there was another big air raid which caused further disaster near our part of the Kemptown area. I can remember that evening very well. We were sitting by a glowing coal and log fire in the sitting room; my father was reading out loud from some memoirs he had just written about his days as a subaltern in the army, spent near the town of Bedford, where he used to go fishing on the Bedfordshire Ouse. I was listening, fairly attentively, to this account, at the same time as, every now and again, having a quick peep out of the window, being careful not to disturb the blackout, to see whether it was snowing or not - there had been a light flurry earlier on, and like the rest of 'our crowd,' I looked forward to there being enough of a covering to go sledging again. The snow didn't arrive however, and by just before ten o'clock, I was in bed and soon asleep. At just after midnight I was awoken in time to hear the siren still going, and mother, Jill and I started making our way down to the basement. The bombs started dropping as we were going down the stairs; they were close enough to make the walls shake and it was extremely frightening! Jill and I didn't bother with the hammocks, but just sat on the chairs beside mother, listening to more bombs falling and heavy gunfire seeming to come from all over the place. I remember my stomach was turning over and over. From the enormous noise coming from our guns - a sound we could recognise - it became obvious that the Germans weren't getting it all their own way, but after a short while everything went quiet, and eventually we heard the all clear. Father, who had arrived in the basement a few minutes after us, because of having to put his false leg on, slowly followed us all back upstairs. "I wonder what's been hit this time?" he said.

"It was definitely pretty close," mother said, "I wonder what the casualty situation is - let's hope there aren't any." she added, still shaking with nerves - as I was! The casualty list, we were soon to find out, was high, and the areas hit were very close to us. Whilst the square had remained almost unscathed again - there were only a few broken windows - it was at the back of the square where the devastation was. Apart from reports from some of the locals we knew, who lived in the vicinity of where the bombings had been, the following appeared in the Evening Argus, 24th February 1944 - the headlines said about working class houses being hit in a south coast raid, and the report went on to say:-

'At least four enemy aircraft were shot down in raids on this country last night. One bomber crashed in the country. The raiding machines were met with a terrific and sustained barrage. A stick of bombs fell on a working class neighbourhood in a south coast town, and at least ten people were killed and several injured.'

The working class neighbourhood mentioned, was the Bennett Road area again; just behind the square. Nine or ten people had been killed in that road alone. Marine Gate had also been hit again, as had Arundel Road, with Wilson's laundry being hit and badly damaged. This laundry had also been damaged by blast during the big raid of May 1943. That morning, after I had gone to school, my parents walked round to the bombed areas and learned that the family that they knew who lived in Bennett Road had not been hurt, but the whole area was a scene of devastation and misery, and they came away very saddened - after letting it be known to some officials, who were at the scene, that there was some temporary accommodation available at number thirteen, should the need arise.

It never did! Everyone who could help, did, and there were offers of help coming in all the time.

This raid is particularly significant to me, because I can't remember ever having to go to the basement again with the express purpose of sheltering from an air raid - it was certainly the last big raid in the Kemptown area. Finally about that raid; concerning the bombing of Wilson's Laundry in Arundel Road. This was the laundry that many residents of the square and nearby schools used - including us, and also, by special contract during the wartime, the armed forces as well. There were tunnels that led from the back of the laundry to the back of some of the houses on the east side of Sussex Square - and the staff used to use these as an air raid shelter. These tunnels were what we called 'the catacombs' - and they led from the back of the houses, including number thirty six, where we used to play sometimes when visiting Timmy. They were originally built so that the residents of that period could get to the coaching stables - where Arundel Road is now. In a letter from Mr.C.W.Wilson, the present managing director of the laundry, he included the following piece of information:-

THE LAUNDRY IN BATTLEDRESS.

In the very early days of the War, our staff were called upon to train for the A.R.P. duties and Decontamination of Civilian and Forces Clothing should the enemy have used Gas Warfare. Fire and First Aid Parties were formed, and the vans and their drivers reported for duty nightly as Ambulances. Plant and equipment were installed and decontamination squads organised. Knitting classes for forces comforts were held weekly by Mrs.Wilson in the staff recreation room. In the laundry itself a change was taking place, less civilian clothing was being sent in, due to the tendency for evacuation in the town, but an ever increasing amount of Naval,Army and Air Force work had to be catered for.

142

In May 1943, the effects of a daylight bombing raid by the enemy were felt in the laundry, then again by a night raid in February 1944.With the exception of a few minor injuries, our staff escaped any serious casualty. Damage to buildings and plant was fairly widespread being mostly broken glass and twisted shafting and piping. With the help of a Company of Canadian troops stationed locally and our own staff, the laundry was on each occasion in full production again within a few days. To our own staff who were always there the next morning whatever the night may have been like, may we say that their devotion to work was exemplary.

During these long War years, Mr. and Mrs.A.W.Wilson carried on the business while their son Mr.C.Wilson, after service with the King's Royal Rifle Corps, transferred his knowledge to Army Laundries, a branch of the Royal Army Ordance Corps. Captain Wilson travelled with Mobile Laundries through North Africa,Italy and North West Europe, eventually finishing off his Army career with a very large Civilian Laundry in Berlin, Germany.

The rest of that winter passed very quietly. The news from abroad, in Europe, was that the fighting in Italy was still raging, but although Rome was still occupied by the Germans it was thought that before long there would be a reckoning in that historical city.

On one of the last days of that term, and just before Easter, I was walking back along the Eastern Road, and hearing voices coming from the other side of the wall outside St.Mary's Hall playing field, I was tempted to look through the same small hole as I had done on that day with Timmy, over a year beforehand and just before the Canadians had arrived. I saw that apart from a few soldiers there, the whole of the field was filled up with small landing craft - similar to the types we had seen in some of the war films that had been on in the past few years. I told my father of this, and he thought that it could be in preparation for the invasion on the continent. It also seemed to tell us that this invasion would be launched from the south east of England - although the actual military movements at that time in the Brighton area - didn't seem to back that up. To this day, with events turning out as they did, and with no invasion setting off from the south east corner, I still puzzle about those landing craft at St.Mary's Hall. One theory about this, is that they were 'dummies' - placed there on purpose - as were, dummy tanks, aeroplanes and other military equipment in various parts of the south east and East Anglia - specifically for giving the impression to any enemy spotter planes, or aircraft on bombing raids or even spies, that this was indeed the area the invasion would come from and that hopefully they would plan their defences accordingly. This was an elaborate hoax - and as it turned out - a successful one. However the more likely reason for the landing craft being there, is that they were the ones the Lake Superiors had used for their landing practice at Piltdown the year before - and now some other regiment was using them.

During the spring of 1944 our thoughts and plans once again turned to the promised second holiday in Surrey. Mothers health at this time was very worrying to us; she had quite frequent spells of sickness now, and also, a small lump which had appeared on her neck was giving her some discomfort and would need to be seen to.

Her illnesses though, were somewhat up and down, and there were plenty of good spells as well as the bad ones. It was becoming increasingly noticeable however that she had to be very careful with what she ate and drank, and this of course led everyone to believe that an ulcer was at the root of things. The doctor, on hearing that X-Rays hadn't shown up anything conclusive, and after giving her another examination, simply instructed her to keep meticulously to her diet and go and enjoy the country air - which hopefully would turn out to be a rest cure for her. Because of this it was decided that we would go to Surrey for a bit longer this time; hopefully getting the best of the summer there. In working out the actual dates for this it meant that it would once again be necessary for Jill and me to miss a couple of weeks schooling at the end of

144

the summer term - not something either of the schools cared for particularly - when eventually told. Jill had some misgivings as well, in case this interfered with the good progress she was making; but I, of course, was very pleased and looked forward to the holiday a little impatiently, even though I did regret that this would also necessitate leaving my friends and the gardens again.

On a sunny day, free from the heavy April showers we had been getting during the Easter holidays, Timmy and I walked over the Downs with the intention of searching for owls nests at Ovingdean; in the area around the farmyard, the church and the grange. We had no idea what an owl's nest looked like, but had read that they nested in barns and similar type buildings. We therefore concentrated our search mainly on the outbuildings of the farm, trying not to wander into areas where we might get caught for trespassing. We didn't find any nests at all in these buildings, and didn't dare to trespass in the grounds of the grange - a place which we still held in some awe because of it's beautiful and mysterious appearance. In a letter from Dulcie Carnaghan, a great grand-daughter of Henry Cowley who had originally bought the house, which had then remained in the Cowley family for 150 years, she says that her grandfather, whilst digging in the garden, had uncovered the entrance to a tunnel that led from there to the church. I have no more information on this - but it certainly smacks of secret hiding places - even smugglers of old. We then decided to explore a small barn about a quarter of a mile up a farm track leading back into the downs; when we had got to within fifty yards of this low building, with an open front to it, we were startled to see two men, probably both in their twenties, coming out of the barn and walking quickly off over the downs in the general direction of Woodingdean. We could see that they were brushing bits of straw and stuff off themselves as they walked - as if they might have been sleeping rough in the straw that the barn contained. We decided not to go any further and returned to the area around the churchyard to continue our quest. After a while, we gave up our search and were about to start the walk back home, when we were stopped by two uniformed policemen who asked us if we had seen two men. We told them what we had just seen, as well as telling them who we were and what we were doing there. Timmy asked them about the men, but they were very non-committal, and just said that they were keen to talk to two suspicious looking characters who had been seen in the area and reported to them; with that, we continued on our way back over the downs.

"They could be looking for German parachutists!" Timmy said dramatically.

"They could be deserters." I said, - remembering what Cyril had once told us about them possibly murdering people, and slightly increasing the pace I was walking at.

"They could be just burglars!" Timmy said - as though we often saw burglars when we were out walking. We were just nearing the golf club when we saw a 'largish' shaggy dog wandering about aimlessly on the downs and not many yards away from us. I called to the dog, "come here boy", - which it did, and we both made a fuss of it. It looked like a slightly smaller version of an English sheepdog, with a bit of something else thrown in; it was in need of a good bath, and smelt a bit. I can still see his large mournful eyes to this day. We walked on, and by the time we had reached Arundel Road the dog was still following us - with neither of us trying to stop it from doing so - in fact I was even encouraging it, and in my mind the idea was already beginning to take shape, that having a pet dog would be a very good idea! I arrived at number thirteen just a few seconds before the dog did; Timmy, had already gone home. My mother, on seeing the dog, who was now standing on the porch, also started to make a fuss of it, but quickly made it quite clear that I wouldn't be able to keep it, because of my grandfather's very strict house rules, which I could remember him saying more than once, "no dogs - cats, yes; but dogs, no!" My father also came out onto the porch to have a look at the dog, who had quickly devoured some bits and pieces my mother had brought out for him and was thoroughly enjoying all the attention he was getting.   Father, after thinking for a while, said - "Blanche, would be the best person to tell us about this - but you never know, someone might be out looking for it right at this moment; in any case, if it does turn out to be a stray, he would be the best person to know about finding him a home!"   My father, I think, was trying to reassure me that the dog wouldn't come to any harm, and told me to run round to St.Marks Place, where Blanche lived, and see if he could come round to number thirteen straight away. Blanche, a dwarf like little man, who did odd jobs for people around the square, including us, and who before the war had been one of the Kemptown enclosures gardeners, was known to be good with all types of animals.   The outcome of it all, was that despite notices going up in various shop windows saying that the dog had been found on the downs near the golf course - no one had come to claim him, and Blanche and his wife were delighted to give him a home themselves. They called him 'Bobby'.   All this particularly pleased me because it meant that not only had he been found a home, but also because Blanche had told me I could come and see the dog whenever I wanted to - and even take him out for walks as well - which I did on quite a few occasions in the years to come.

At the beginning of the summer term of 1944, I joined the junior school scout troop, and can remember my mother taking me to the scout shop in Guildford Road, just near the station, to get equipped with all the required stuff, including; a whistle, lanyard, woggle, trousers, shirt and scarf; not forgetting a stave and also of course the pointed hat, which we put four dents into to make it look like the hats the 'mounties' wore.

There was some good hot weather during the May of that year and on May 29th. a temperature of 91 degrees Fahrenheit was recorded at Horsham in Sussex. This was an all time record for May, and that record may still stand to this day. The weather in those early days of June became a bit unsettled, but we didn't know just how crucial it was at that time for the elements to be kind, and certainly for the sea to be calm, or reasonably so. On Monday June 5th. we were ignorant of the fact that because of inclement weather, a huge armada that had been set to sail from the shores of Great Britain that day, had had to stay where it was. By the following day the weather had improved enough for the invasion of France to take place.

During that memorable day of Tuesday June 6th. 1944, we started getting reports of the invasion on the beaches of Normandy - quite early, and the country, including us at school, was kept informed of the situation frequently throughout the day. The headlines of the Argus that evening were:- "MIGHTY AIR LAND AND SEA ATTACK." It also reported that tanks had been landed in France, and our thoughts immediately went back to all the tanks we had seen on manoeuvres, and of the men we had known so well during the months they were training in the Brighton area during 1943. We didn't really know even if they were involved as yet, but they were in our thoughts none the less - as also, were various relatives and friends. We thought that Uncle Charles would probably be in the thick of things, and amongst many others, my godfather, Alec Chalmers, now a captain in the Royal Gloucester's, would also probably be somewhere near to the spearhead of the attack.

In the bottom gardens that evening, Janine, Peter, myself and a few of the others, gathered at the horseshoe and instead of finding some game to play, we talked, and the names of many of our relatives and friends cropped up in this conversation. "Uncle Keith will probably have been on one of the ships taking part in the invasion"; Janine said. He was a lieutenant in the royal navy. Several of the others mentioned relatives that they thought might be involved - including Peter - who said, "my father will probably be involved as well!" - I remember wondering about this, as he was a dentist in the R.A.F.; but then, of course, I thought they'd

148

need dentists over there as well. After a while we made our way up to the top gardens, hoping to be able to listen to some of the adult conversation going on about the day's happenings. A small group of men were gathered around my father who was sitting in his deck chair, not far from 'our tree'. They were talking about the report in the Argus about the day's happenings. Just under the big headlines it went on to say:-

"Preceded and covered by a mighty bombardment from sea and air, allied troops today swept up the beaches at various points in northern France. Latest reports are encouraging and state that good progress has been made and that our troops are 'slashing in land'. The first official news came in a statement desribed as, 'communique number one,' from Supreme Headquarters Allied Expeditionary Force, (S.H.A.E.F.), saying naval forces, supported by strong air forces, began landing allied armies this morning on the northern coast of France. In this brief manner the United Nations, their enemies and the people of neutral nations were told that 'D.Day' had arrived and that the first stage in the liberation of Europe had begun."

As the next few days unfolded, the news came through, thick and fast, of allied advances and occasional setbacks; of very fierce fighting and of course, sadly, heavy casualties. On the whole though, the news was encouraging, but nearly everyone we knew, either seemed to know, or were related to, someone who would probably be involved in the fighting, and the consequential worrying was prevalent.

On June 13th. a new and terrifying weapon, the V.1. 'Flying Bomb', or 'Doodlebug', as it was better known, became the spearhead of a new German offensive on this country, and this of course increased the already heavy 'worryload.' According to the records, - of the ten V.1.'s sent over the channel that day, just four managed to find land.   The first of these crashed down on the village of Swanscombe, in Kent, another one also came down in Kent, at Sevenoaks, and another at Bethnal Green. The second one

149

to come down though, wasn't very far from Brighton, - at Cuckfield.   In the days and weeks that followed that horrific first day of these deadly missiles, we quite often saw them going over while we were in the gardens, and if up a tree at the time, we would very quickly scramble down.   We were fortunate that they always missed us, and flew on to some less fortunate area, making their unmistakable deep engine noise and showing their fiery tails as they disappeared from view. Although many did drop in country areas and towns in the home counties, Hitler had ordered that London was to be the prime target - and it certainly was! By the end of June approximately 2000 of these devastating weapons had been sent across the channel, and this set a big problem for the air force and those on the ground manning the guns, who were trying to shoot them down before they could do much damage. In trying to work out the best way of destroying these machines, it was found out that they flew over at a height of between 2000 and 3000 feet; this made it difficult for the gunners, because it was too high for the light guns and too low for the heavy guns.   They could also reach speeds of up to 400 m.p.h. before the engine suddenly stopped - then a silence - then a whooshing sound, and then the inevitable explosion. It was decided that by using new kinds of shells and positioning many more guns in a line from just near Newhaven to just beyond Dover, that this would give the guns unrestricted field of fire at the V.1.'s coming in from the channel; with the shells and destroyed V.1's falling harmlessly into the sea, this would also give the R.A.F. a better go at them as they flew from the coast to the North Downs - where they would run into more defenses - in the shape of large numbers of barrage balloons.

The pilots of our fighter planes soon discovered that it was hazardous to shoot down one of these missiles from too close behind; the safe distance being about 200 yards - certainly no less!

Some pilots though, if they had run out of ammunition, would fly close to the doodlebug and place one of the fighters wings against one of the missile's - and 'tip it over,' - always bearing in

150

mind where it was likely to come to earth. Towards the end of July, the ground and air defences against the V.1. were enormous and the threat from this horrific type of warfare lessened considerably. Reviewing this subject, it was thought at the time, and still is thought, that if Hitler had started using these weapons a couple of weeks beforehand, and if he had targeted the Portsmouth - Southampton areas, instead of London, D-Day, the invasion of France, wouldn't have taken place when it did and operation Overlord would have been delayed at least; thereby changing the history books.

In the middle of July 1944, with the V.1's still occasionally passing overhead, and with my mother very much in need of a rest cure in the country, we once again made our way to Brighton station with all our luggage for the journey to Surrey. We were met at Dorking station by 'Jones', with the car, and driven to Bunts Place for this, much looked forward to, second holiday at the farm. Cousin Grace seemed fine, but told us that a few of the doodlebugs had come down - "not too many miles away, and every time I hear one of the blasted things, it nearly gives me heart failure!" We were all soon billeted in the same bedrooms as before and we once again had the library as our living room. My mother's health improved a little over the weeks in Surrey, but while we were there she had had the lump on her neck lanced, and although it was found to be some sort of a cyst, there was apparently a complication and she was advised to see her own doctor as soon as she arrived back in Brighton. This altered our arrangements and it was decided that we would end our holiday earlier than had been arranged and return to Sussex Square on Saturday August 26th. Although I was enjoying the Surrey countryside very much, I now looked forward to more time than I thought I would have during those summer holidays, back in the company of my friends. The day before we returned to Brighton I walked around the farm and nearby fields and woods, having a last look round; I also made a fuss of some of the animals, and said good-bye to the Jones and

Cook families. Just before leaving Bunts Place the next day, we also said our goodbyes to Annie and Janie. Cousin Grace, after giving us an open invitation to come again whenever we wanted, bid us farewell, and we then left by car for Dorking and the train to Brighton.

That evening, unpacked and settled back into number thirteen we listened to the news, which told of the imminent liberation of Paris. Also, in that day's Evening Argus, under the heading, 'NOTHING TO REPORT,' it said:

A ministry of home communique this morning simply states: "Up to 7 o/clock this morning there has been nothing to report and there has now been a lull of twenty four hours in flying bomb activity!" We had noticed a lack of activity from these dreaded V1's a few days before we left off from Surrey, and this report now gave everyone the hope that we had seen the last of them.

That evening I climbed up to my favourite perch in 'our tree'; it was nice to see the sea again and I noticed that there were two smallish boats settled on the calm water not more than a mile from the shore; it looked like the people in them were fishing. That night I thought about my father being able to fish in the sea again, and me going with him. There had been quite a bit of talk on this subject, and it was the general opinion, that before long, any mines that had been placed along the shores, would soon be cleared, and with any luck, before the year was out, we might once again be able to enjoy the freedom of the beaches.

Ovingdean Grange (late Thirties).
("The boy in the picture is Dennis Filkins – Dulcie Carnaghan's
brother".)

Ovingdean Manor Hall School. The Canadian Tank Corps were stationed here – The concrete blocks the tanks stood on – are still there.

Wilson Laundry (Arundel Road), after bombing February 23rd
1944.

Cricketing Uncle with some team members Sussex CCC. Tate, Jim
Langridge, Gilligan, Duleep, Lance Knowles, Bowley, Cox.

St Wulfrans, Ovingdean.

Piltdown Lake. Where the Canadians did Landing Craft Training.

CHAPTER ELEVEN.

The beaches - are they safe now? -- An eventful fishing outing.

The day after our arrival back from Surrey, we got an invitation from Edie Whitehead to join her and her family for a picnic on a beach at South Lancing. This invitation was very coincidental, considering my thoughts about being able to use the beaches again. We immediately accepted the invitation, and at mid-day, caught the bus from Poole Valley. The beach we were going to was one of the first in the south east to be 'unofficially' reopened to the public - in other words, the local authorities were 'turning a blind eye' to stopping anyone from using them, despite the fact that there was no actual authorisation from the war office, and consequently, if you turned up there - no-one would turn you away! "It was," Edie had told mother on the phone, "quite safe, and for some reason hadn't been mined - at least that's what I've been told." she added.

We arrived at the beach on that hot Sunday afternoon, after an interesting bus ride from Poole Valley, to find it completely packed. There were people swimming, paddling, picnicking, sunbathing and a few ardent anglers actually trying to fish amongst the multitudes! We spent an enjoyable afternoon there, during which, I spent most of the time in the water, and even witnessed one of the fishermen catching a flat fish - how he'd managed to cast out amongst all those people - I can't imagine. None of the Brighton beaches had been opened by then; or at least, as far as I can remember or ascertain, none of them had. Later on, on Saturday September 9th. the following appeared in the Argus: "Brighton beach not open this year." It went on to say:

"Brighton beach will not be open to the public this year and it will probably be next summer before access is granted, meanwhile the town's emergency committee have approached several government departments in the hope of securing a 'super detector' to clear the beaches of mines.

The mayor, Cllr.B.Dutton-Bryant said today, "we want to make the beaches as safe as it is humanly possible to make them, and we are hoping that the winter gales and shifting sands will help to explode some of the mines." I remember that my parents were very worried about Mr.Dutton-Bryant's statement, and I should think plenty of other people were too!   In retrospect, I think that hoping for rough seas and shifting sands to explode the mines, must have put a lot of people off going to the beaches again for a very long time. As it turned out we did hear differing rumours of people being blown up by mines that the detectors had failed to find; but the real facts about this are unobtainable. What actually happened though, was that once the beaches did reopen, most people simply trusted that all the mines had been cleared and started using the beaches accordingly - and that included us!

The war office in a communique to local councils in the areas from Great Yarmouth, round the coast to Littlehampton, had given permission for the barbed wire to go, and it is believed it was up to the individual councils, whether they wanted to do the clearing up of the beaches themselves, and claim compensation from the war office for any damage done, or, wait until the army could come and do it - which might mean quite a long wait!

My father hadn't accompanied us to South Lancing for the picnic, but had listened with interest to our account of the afternoon - especially about the people fishing from the beach. He told us how much he was looking forward to being able to fish from the beaches below the square again, and now that I was that much older, he promised that he would take me with him, allowing me the use of one of his rods, after he had tried out all the lines again - I very much looked forward to that. Throughout the war years he had made sure that his fishing lines and rods and old star-back reels, were kept oiled and ready for use at the first opportunity. Although the news that the beaches weren't to reopen in the

Brighton area until the summer of 1945, was to say the least, depressing; I remember father saying, " - such reports aren't infallible and there could still be the chance that some of them might be open by the early spring."

On September 9th. the news came through of another type of flying bomb - the V2 - which was far more devastating than the V1. The first of these had exploded in England the day before; but thankfully, we never saw or heard anything of these horrific weapons - which were apparently powerful enough to demolish a whole street!

At the beginning of the new term, the news started coming through of the big airborne attack and subsequent fierce fighting at Arnhem - this of course had the whole family thinking of Uncle Charles - who would more than likely be in the thick of it. My mother made a point of spending as much time as possible with Aunt Daphne, who, although worried sick, was bearing up remarkably well considering all the worry of not knowing anything. When the news did eventually come through about the raid being the distastrous failure that it was - and with no news of Uncle Charles at all - the atmosphere at number thirteen was, to put it mildly - 'uptight.' Sometime later my aunt was officially informed that her husband had been wounded at Arnhem, and that, as a result of his wounds, his left leg had been amputated from below the knee and that he would soon be sent to a hospital in England; other than that he was reported to be alright. The news that he was alive was all that Aunt Daphne had been wanting to hear, and relieved beyond description, she opened a bottle of scotch and shared it with my parents - my mother just having a sip or two - but father and her, eventually emptying the bottle, and going to their respective beds that night - "quite merry," - as Jill told me the next morning.

During that term, Peter and I made several more visits to the college cinematograph society to see a variety of old films. We enjoyed these performances - not only for the films, but also, the unpredictability of any breakdowns, during which, the ensuing pandemomium could also be quite entertaining. My school work however, still left something to be desired, and my father told me that if my Latin and French didn't improve considerably by the end of the spring term, he would have no alternative but have to pay for extra tuition for me, and, knowing that I knew that this would have to take place in my leisure time, he must have felt quite confident that I would try to avoid this at all costs!

Towards the end of November, on a cold and gloomy Saturday morning, a group of us were playing in the top gardens when we saw that some policemen were making sure that no-one could get too close to the easterly end of the watertank. The arrival of an ambulance, and some army personal with one man in a sort of "underwater suit" - who we saw going into the water - immediately had us all keenly watching what was going on ; we were standing just near the path on that side of the gardens. Timmy soon joined us - as did my sister and some of her friends - there were quite a crowd of us. We kept our distance as the police instructed us to. Quite soon, we were horrified to see they had recovered the body of a small boy - probably not ten years of age - from the murky depths of the water tank. We hadn't any idea who he was, but were later told that a boy had gone missing from the Whitehawk area the day before. I shall always remember the sight of that boy's body, turned 'blue - grey' by the cold water, and totally rigid. We had gone through all the bombing without any fatalities actually in the square, and now this tragic accident - in something that had been put there to help preserve lives and property, should there have been fires during the hostilities. It was sad for everyone, and there were many tears shed for that unfortunate small boy and his parents.

On another cold dry day, just over a week before Christmas, a familiar figure arrived on the doorstep of number thirteen, he hadn't got a key with him, but my Uncle Charles was very quickly made to feel at home, not only by us, but also of course a deliriously happy Daphne, carrying their two year old son. On that same afternoon there was a telephone call from my grandmother in Penrith, "Little-Ma," saying that she and grandpa would also be home for Christmas; "home permanently," she had added. So, with the air raids, hopefully a thing of the past, and the family now nearly all coming together again, the prospects for a happy Christmas and a peaceful new year, were looking very good indeed; the added pleasure for me was that the next day was the first day of the Christmas Holidays. Uncle Charles hadn't yet been fitted with a false leg and for the time being was getting about on crutches - with the trouser leg pinned up. On the second day of his Christmas leave, he and my father popped down to the Rock Inn, for a drink or two before lunch. When they returned they told us that the landlord, 'Dave Caplin,' had told them it was the first time he had ever seen two gentlemen, 'legless,' after just two light ales each!

With the holidays now stretching in front of us, Jill told me that this year she would, after all, be going carol singing again, and asked if my friends and I would like to make up a large group; the idea being to go as far as Roedean Crescent,where we knew people; this is just near Roedean School. We would also of course go to all the usual places. We readily accepted this invitation, and immediately resolved that any practice that year wouldn't be necessary.

With my grandparents due to arrive home on the 21st.of December, Charles, Daphne and Charles junior had vacated the balcony flat at number thirteen and had gone to stay with a relative of Charles', who lived nearby. Early on the Thursday afternoon, Little Ma and Grandpa stepped out of a taxi outside number thirteen, and with the driver and all of us helping them with their luggage and numerous exciting looking parcels, they were quickly reinstalled in their own flat, in their own house. That night there was a small family party in the verandah flat, during which, my grandfather - on hearing that I had been getting plenty of practice on the snooker table - challenged me to a game; saying that, "after all this time he'd be a little rusty!" This encouraged me to think I would show him a thing or two that night - but at the end of the game I came out decidedly second best, and had to admit I had come up against someone who was still more than a match for me!

There were quite a few parties on the run up to that Christmas, and at one in particular, at Timmy's house, where his mother, Monha, held a party to celebrate - "a Christmas with no air raids at last," - I drank something a bit stronger than the usual lemonade or ginger beer. Timmy had acquired a flagon of cider and a packet of cigarettes, and with these and a couple of glasses we disappearded into the 'catacombs,' leaving the others to get on with it. For the next hour or so we sipped the cider whilst entertaining one another with games of ghostly hide and seek, in the narrow passages, and afterwards, some elaborate impersonations from the films we had seen - including a very good one by Timothy of Sydney Greenstreet in 'Casablanca.' The best that I could manage was a rather poor 'Alan Ladd,' with a cigarette - which nearly choked me - dangling from the corner of my mouth. Timmy went on to excel himself as 'Peter Lorre,' who he masterfully managed to make himself look just like, and the evening ended hilariously and enjoyably.

A party of sixteen of us went carol singing that Christmas eve. My mother had given me a large paper bag to put in my pocket, saying, "this time if you get anything you can't eat – put it in the bag, and try to keep it so it doesn't get all squashed up!" We did very well that evening and the men from the workhouse were given the lion's share of this in both tobacco and cash.

There was quite a lot of socialising that festive season, and just after Christmas a party of us went to see Bertram Montague's pantomime, 'Dick Whittington,' at the Hippodrome, which I enjoyed, but would have liked better if 'Jill Manners' had been in it. The day after this we went to the cinema to see Michael Wilding in, 'English Without Tears,' this was alright, but the second feature, a Sherlock Holmes film, with Basil Rathbone and Nigel Bruce, called, 'The Scarlet Claw,' - I thought was brilliant, and ranked it almost as good as 'The Hound of the Baskervilles.' Included in those days of holiday entertainment, there was one outing that was different as well as enjoyable; this was a pantomime on ice at the sports stadium in West Street. It was called, 'Snow Flake and the Penguins.' This was Aunt Daphne's treat, or rather, because of her ice skating connnections, she had been given some free tickets. I can remember being taken to some of the shows she appeared in before the war, and particularly remember being thrilled by the spectacular barrel jumping and other daring feats, of a gentleman called -'Red McCarthy.'

1945 came in on a mildish note, and on Thursday January 18th. we returned to school after a memorable holiday. Later that day the winds got up to gale force and continued like that right into the next day - all the time getting colder. The first snow of that year fell during the night of the 19th, and we had quite a good covering everywhere for about a couple of weeks. At the week-ends the sledges once again saw the light of day, and there were several outings to the downs above East Brighton park By the beginning of March we had the full use of the bottom gardens again, and with the barbed wire having been taken away, we could now get down to the tunnel again. Some of the beaches had re-opened; but many - including the ones below the square - remained closed until thoroughly checked and re-checked for any mines that might remain concealed on them. There were reports that on some of the beaches between Ovingdean and Rottingdean, good catches of bass were being made. My father, on hearing this, said that we would give this a try when the weather was better, probably early in April, and at Rottingdean, where he had fished many times before the war.

Apart from the news of continuing advances into Germany,

there was also some good news from the far east. My father knew two of the officers in the Royal Sussex Regiment and on Tuesday March the thirteenth, the following appeared in the Argus concerning that regiment. "Royal Sussex took hill 800 - brilliant action in Burma." It goes on to describe how they had helped capture a communication centre. Items of news like these were particularly heartening, because although the war in Europe was nearly over, the hostilities in the far east were still continuing, and some people we knew still had relatives out there, who they hadn't heard from for some considerable time.

On the radio on Thursday 12th. of April, the news came through of the death of President Roosevelt. The next day the Argus carried a front page report of Mr.Churchill's tribute to, "this great man," which included his words: "who's friendship for the cause of freedom and for the causes of the weak and the poor have won him immortal renown."

On Saturday the 14th. of April, a pleasant sunny day, my mother decided that as 'spring was in the air,' it would be a good idea to go for a country walk that afternoon, instead of going to the pictures; she decided that we would go somewhere different this time. My sister already had different plans for that afternoon and my father, of course, no longer came on these country rambles, because of his leg; so, early that afternoon it was just mother and me who got off the bus at the Sussex Pad Hotel at North Lancing, to follow the road that we had walked several times before, when going swimming in the river Adur. We joined the river near our usual swimming spot, and walked for what seemed like miles, and probably was, along the river bank towards Bramber. In the middle of the afternoon we came to a backwater where there were several houseboats moored to the bank, and also, a couple of caravans parked nearby to a small road. On one of the houseboats we saw a very big woman who was wearing the largest earings I have ever seen - she looked like a gypsy to me; she was hanging out some washing on a makeshilft clothes line on the boat. She and mother soon got into conversation, and before long we had an invitation to go on board and have a look around and a cup of tea. I wasn't very keen on this idea, but didn't say anything, and duly followed my mother and the 'gypsy' lady down the steps and into the small cabin below. Lying on a bunk bed just beside a table, on which there were several empty Guinness bottles, was a large, unshaven man, snoring away and completely oblivious to the fact that he had visitors. With a half hearted, but well aimed kick at the slumbering man, the lady called out loudly – "come on 'Arry' - make yerself useful, - got some people 'ere come in for a cuppa!" 'Arry,' quickly sat bolt upright, - then stretching himself whilst looking at us and mumbling some sort of an apology, - went and filled up a large black kettle and put it on a small stove nearby. During the conversation that my mother had with this lady, it turned out that she and her husband were part of a small travelling fair that was due to take to the roads again that summer, for the first time since before the war. She told us, a little sadly, that before long the boat would be put into "mothballs" for the summer, and they would be using one of the caravans we could see parked outside. She said, she would once again be telling fortunes and that 'Arry' did general maintainance work around the fairground. When we had finished our tea, and just before we left off, the 'gypsy' lady, looked at my mothers palm, and, amongst other things, told her that she would be going on a long journey; but that it was a necessary one, and everything would be alright! With that, we said our goodbyes, and rejoining the path by the river bank, we started to make our way to the nearest bus stop for the journey home. I noticed that my mothers face, which had been rather pale of late, had distinctly got more colour in it, and although we didn't talk much on the way home, she looked a lot happier than I had seen her for quite some time. The next day, Sunday April 15th. was her thirty ninth birthday, and we celebrated this quietly, with my grandparents joining us for tea.

Also on April 15th - on the radio; a war reporter named

167

Richard Dimbleby, gave a live commentary while walking around a place opened for the first time to reporters; it was called 'Belsen.' The descriptions he made, in his memorable voice, of that hellish concentration camp - are difficult to forget! The horror of it all, as it began to sink in - is beyond adequate description, so I will leave it; but my final words on this are that, "I pray we'll never see or hear the likes of it again!"

On Monday 16th. April 1945, we had our first sea fishing outing since before the war - it turned out to be an eventful one! Early that morning I had been sent to collect a large tin containing six peeler crabs from Silverlocks the fishing tackle shop in Duke Street. A little later, my father, Peter and I took the bus to Rottingdean; the arrangement being that my mother would meet us there later and bring some picnic stuff with her. It was a sunny and surprisingly warm day for that time of the year, and quite 'grilling' where we had decided to fish - about two hundred yards west of the main promenade, which was sheltered from the offshore breezes by the steep cliffs. There was however a nasty swell on the water, and the breakers every now and again smacked hard against the beach wall sending clouds of spray right over the top - and not very far from where my father had made his first cast from. That first cast - with one of his old star back reels with pre-war 'string like' green line on it - checked and only went about twenty yards out. He decided to leave it where it was for a while. After a few minutes, Peter and I, who were keenly watching the rod, noticed that the line seemed to be 'swimming' back into the wall just below us; I told my father of this and he straight away picked up the rod, reeled in the slack line, and struck -- he was immediately into a good fish! This fish - a large bass - quickly came to the surface and then disappeared again, and for several minutes my father played it - during which time quite a crowd had gathered. Realising that the old line was probably not strong enough to haul the fish up over the wall, he called out for one of us to run to the steps at the easterly end of the beach - about thirty yards away - where he would drag the fish to;

168

it was where the tide didn't reach and there were just the pebbles. Peter was quicker off the mark than me, and without heeding what my father had said, raced along the beach to where the water - now and again - still reached as far as the wall - only briefly leaving the pebbles uncovered. He grabbed the line instead of the fish, and that immediately broke, and in the next instant a large wave took both the fish and Peter out to sea. This was a dreadful moment, the crowds just stood there gaping, my father with his one leg could do nothing and I was still on the beach near the steps. Fortunately, a quick thinking soldier, leapt over the wall and pulled Peter to safety. My father, after profusely thanking the soldier, who then quickly disappeared into the crowd, told me to get Peter home as quickly as possible and gave me the money for a taxi to do so - saying that he would wait for my mother to arrive and then come home with her. I duly delivered Peter, soaking wet, but apart from that, none the worse for his adventure, to his home and then went home myself. Later that afternoon, when we were all back at home again, my father said that at the time the fishing line had broken, the fish was probably dead, and with the fishing tackle and lead weight still attached to it, it might be found in one of the rock pools at low tide that evening.

At just after six o'clock, we returned to Rottingdean, this time with Jill and my mother coming with us, but not Peter - who, thankfully, was perfectly alright. After an enjoyable half an hour of searching, we found the dead fish in a pool at the end of one of the breakwaters. I didn't tell anyone, but I secretly felt sorry for the fish. We carried this 'trophy' up to the White Horse Hotel where the landlord weighed it for us. It scaled in at six pounds and twelve ounces. The next day we ate this tasty fish; having it baked and stuffed. We invited Peter to join us, but he declined, - saying, "I don't really like fish." That was the first time I had ever known Peter to refuse a meal! A few months after this incident my father wrote an article about it, and it was duly accepted and printed in a small monthly magazine called 'Angling.'

On Thursday 19th. of April a small party had been arranged for Jill who was celebrating her sixteenth birthday, and, as this was strictly for her own friends, I was glad to accept an offer of tea with a friend of mine who lived in the Queens Park district of Brighton. Peter Collier, who was the same age as me, and had joined Brighton College Junior School a year or so after me, was the son of an army major and well known opera singing mother.   On that afternoon, before going out to see what we could get up to in the park, Peter said he had something to show me, which he had hidden in their garden shed.   From under a pile of old junk he pulled out a small box which was full of live rifle bullets; on asking him where he had got them from, I got an evasive answer, and pursued the subject no further - but on asking him what he was going to do with them - he said, "I'll soon show you!" He then placed one of the bullets into a small vice, and with a pair of plyers, took the actual bullet head away from the case, - so you could see what was inside the casing. Leaving the contents where they were, he neatly hammered the opening shut, then, with some sticking tape, he attached an 18 inch piece of string to the case.   This of course made it bottom heavy, when suspended, with the detonator, of course, being at the bottom. He then did exactly the same with a second bullet, and putting them both in his pocket, he said "now - follow me!" We then went out onto the street and walked towards the park.   At a place a bit further on, where there were just some houses and no people about at the time, we stopped, and Peter 'swung' one of the bullets high into the air, - he quickly followed this with the other one - then within a second or two of one another - there were two extremely loud bangs from the detonators connecting with the hard road when they came down; it was at this point that Peter and I made ourselves scarce from the scene, and I noticed as I ran, that people were already coming to their windows. In actual fact this wasn't the first time I had seen this happen. When the Canadians had been in the square, someone we knew had acquired some bullets, and had done exactly the same thing with

170

them.   In those days the security arrangements for guarding the trucks, in which a lot of live ammunition was kept, was 'insecure' - to say the least.   During the months the Canadians were here, there were many stories of youngsters being found in possession of various types of 'arsenals' - however, if a rifle went missing - then all hell broke loose until it was found; bullets though, were apparently difficult to keep a check on!

On April 30th, two days after it was reported that Mussolini had been 'executed' by partisans, the news came through that Hitler was dead. Needless to say, there were no tears shed for him! This was the last nail in the coffin of the Third Reich, and everyone's hopes were raised in the expectancy of an imminent announcement of the end of the war. When on May the second it was announced that the Germans had finally capitulated in Italy and that the Russians had taken Berlin, our wireless set was left on for most of the time, and we eagerly awaited the 'overdue' news of the end of the war; with the broadcast, probably to be made by Winston Churchhill. Before this news did eventually come through - in another five days - we had a bit of family news that especially pleased my grandparents and my mother. During the morning of May the third, Uncle Charles arrived at number thirteen to tell us that Daphne was expecting again and that thay were also in the process of buying the house that they had set their hearts on in Cumberland Road, near Preston Park. This news certainly perked my mother up; she had been 'down in the dumps' with further health problems, and a new and stricter diet which she said, "doesn't allow me to eat or drink any of the things that I really enjoy!" She had been to the doctors yet again, and apparently even x-rays hadn't shown up anything definite; she had also taken a second opinion, but no-one seemed able to give an exact diagnosis.

On the Saturday of that week;   looking better than she had done for quite some time, mother said that she was going to go on one of her special country walks - this time to the downs near

Patcham for a walk that she and my father used to make back in the nineteen-twenties and thirties. Jill once again had made her own arrangements, but I had managed to persuade Peter to come with us, and so, on that warm, sunny, but windy afternoon, we took the bus from Pool Valley, and alighted about half a mile past the Black Lion at Patcham, and started our walk in the nearby countryside. All went well until we were on our way back down towards the road again, when mother quietly told me, she had to sit down for a while. She had gone very white, and then - quite suddenly - she fainted! I had seen her do this once before, but that had been at home; it was all very frightening, and I felt in a hopeless position - not knowing quite what to do. There was no-one else about, just Peter - and he didn't seem to understand what was going on - however, I was just about to ask him to run to some houses I could see near the road - about a quarter of a mile away - when she managed to sit up, and, although still very pale, said she felt better now, and that I was to stay close to her and we'd go and catch the bus back home. I sat beside her on that worrying bus journey; as I did on the journey from Poole Valley back to Sussex Square - each time with Peter sitting on his own - not quite understanding what was going on, but none the less enquiring whether everything was alright. By the time we had got indoors, mother said that she felt much better now and that she was even quite hungry! That night I slept uneasily, and the next day - on waking up with a stomach ache - and complaining of it; I was allowed the day off school.   In those days we used to go to school on Saturday mornings, so I had that off as well. I returned to school on the Monday, and on that day it was announced that Admiral Doenitz, the new German Fuhrer, had said it was useless to fight on any further and that he had ordered the unconditional surrender of all the German fighting troops.   At this point there was some disappointment that Winston Churchill hadn't made an official announcement, and as the Argus put it, with everyone hanging on for his announcement and prepared for the victory in Europe day celebrations, - Brighton was "all dressed up with nowhere to go;" - however on Tuesday May the eighth, Mr.Churchill announced that "hostilities in Europe officially end one minute after midnight tonight."

"It is difficult to put into words how one feels at this moment in time." My father said. That day there was a mixture of tears and laughter; of memories and of hopes and new ideas. To crown the day for us, - especially mother and my grandparents, the news also came through that her brother, our Uncle Jimmy, would be home safe and sound in the next few days! The atmosphere seemed to be electrically charged, and emotions ran very high indeed. A little later my father told Jill and me that we could stay up until whatever time we wanted to that night. He also said that he wouldn't be going down town to see the celebrations himself, as the crowds would probably be immense, and that would mean that there would be a lot of jostling about, and his leg wouldn't be able to take it. Jill accordingly made her own arrangements for that evening, and I was left wondering what I would do. A little later, Peter's mother offered to take Peter and me to see the celebrations at the clock tower; " -- if we can get anywhere near it!" she said. My parents, who had been invited to a party with friends at the top of the square, said that I was to have a good meal before I left off; mother also added that as it was probably going to be a chilly evening, I would have to 'wrap up' quite well. Peter and I could hardly contain ourselves with all the excitement, and it was arranged that we would leave off from his place at eight o.clock - it was to be an evening we were never likely to forget!

CHAPTER TWELVE

Victory celebrations. – Peace at last.

M y mother's weather forecast for that night turned out to be correct, and we were glad that we had come adequately dressed for the evening, which soon became quite cool. We left off from the square at just after eight o'clock, and decided to take the seafront route down town. We noticed that there were a few 'white horses' forming on the crests of small waves in a slightly choppy looking sea, which was beginning to get stirred up by the freshening winds. During that day we had tried to buy some fireworks, but were unsuccessful in purchasing anything more more spectacular than a box of Bengal lights each, from the half crowns our parents had given us earlier on for this purpose, so we both had some change left to spend during the evening. We hoped that once it got dark we would see plenty of fireworks going off, and we weren't to be disappointed. We saw, as we passed by the Palace Pier, the gap about halfway down it, which had been made - rather drastically we had thought at the time - in case of invasion. It was thought that a pier such as this would make a good landing place for the enemy, or, as we children imaginatively liked to think, a good place for spies to be landed when being secretly smuggled into the country. This pier was to remain closed until 1946 - unlike the West pier which had had a similar gap 'cut' into it, and which was repaired and reopened in 1945.

We now noticed that the crowds on the streets were getting larger all the time, and now and again we stopped to watch impromptu 'turns' performed by merrymakers and intended as general entertainment. Red, white and blue rosettes or scarves or hats or combinations of them, were worn by practically everyone - including us. The street lights came on just as dusk was descending, and this was the first time that this had happened since the beginning of the war. The blackout of course had been over for quite some time, but with this added light, the normally darkened streets became brightly lit from a myriad of lights of varying intensity. The pubs, with their doors wide open and their customers flowing out onto the streets, were all doing a roaring trade, and here and there, people took to dancing on the pavements and on the roads; through which, no cars could pass. Snake-like lines of people wearing funny hats and grasping each other's waists, did the 'Hokey-cokey' - winding their way through the shoulder to shoulder thronging crowds, who readily made way for them to go unimpeded in their revelry. The fireworks soon started, with rockets zooming into the air from all over the place, and screams coming from excited young ladies as penny bangers exploded - sometimes perilously close to them. Some of the more agile and adventurous ones from the huge crowd even climbed up the clock tower - a few actually reaching the top!

We stood at the door of Hyman's the ladies hairdressers in West Street; a small business owned by one of Peter's uncles. Peter's mother held tightly onto our hands, in fear of losing us amongst the bustling crowds. Just for a while all barriers came down in a show of happiness and exultation, and it seemed that everybody spoke to everybody. We stayed where we were for over an hour, and then, a little reluctantly, we made our way down to the seafront again to begin the walk back to Kemptown and home.

After passing the crowds that had gathered on the seafront near the Palace Pier, we walked past the aquarium and onto the middle walk that lies between Madeira Drive and Marine Parade, and is known as Madeira Terrace; we soon found ourselves more or less on our own and away from the general hubbub of the festivities.   As we walked along this pleasant promenade, we struck our Bengal lights, which quickly flared green or red - lasted just a few seconds - and then went out.   From time to time rockets soared into the sky from nearby, eventually exploding into showers of bright golden stars. On arriving back at the square, and after saying goodnight to Peter and his mother, I made my way up to number twenty three, and the flat the flat where the Hodgkins used to live, and which was occupied by friends of my parents - Nicky Marcy and his wife Noreen. The party was in full swing and I noticed that Jill was there with her boyfriend, Alec. I made my way through the 'wall to wall' guests, carefully clutching a large glass of lemonade, and squatted on the carpet near to the armchair where mother sat. With the knowledge that I wasn't going to have to get up for school the next morning, I sat back, determined to keep awake and watch all that was going on. I listened to the loud talk and happy laughter of celebrating adults - with their cups running over - who, without reserve, were letting their hair down and having a whale of a time! Once again the drinks flowed generously - a bit too generously in some cases - including my father's, as was to be very evident the next morning! At well past midnight we made our way back to number thirteen, and very quickly, to bed and instant sleep. The night had certainly been one to remember, but what I remember the most about it was the conviviality between everyone - wherever we went, it was as if we were all part of a huge family party, and I surpose - in a way - we were!

There were more celebrations during that week, but for us, nothing more on the scale of that night. On the Saturday we went down as far as Castle Square, walking along the seafront again to get there. The lights along the front were specially lit up for that week-end, but because of having to save on power, it was announced that after that, they would stay off until July 15th, in order to conserve energy. It was also announced that double British summer time would end on that date. After that week-end the 'party', for us, was over! School carried on as normal, the rationing also carried on - and would do for quite a few years to come. In the meantime we waited and wondered about the conclusion of the war in the far east.

The following Sunday, whilst playing in the top gardens, one of the newcomers to our crowd, a girl called Jacqueline, who had recently moved into number twelve, next door to us, was talking about her life in India and about all the 'trophies' that they had bought back with them from that country, and which now adorned the walls of the flat she lived in with her sister and parents. I was intrigued and asked her if I could see them sometime; she agreed, and said that as her parents were out now, we could go and see them straight away. I was shown up into the most luxuriously furnished flat that I had ever seen. There were tapestries on the walls and several pictures of jungle scenes, which I liked very much. There were also the heads of some animals, which, although also intriguing me, I found 'uncomfortable' to look at. The star of this show of extravaganza and indifference to the welfare of animals, was a huge tiger's head and skin, which lay on the luxurious, thickly piled carpet in the centre of the room; it had it's mouth wide open showing it's very large teeth, as if it was permanently snarling - which of course it was! There was a desk in the corner of the room, and, in a special holder, there was an assortment of quill pens. Jacqueline told me she loved writing and drawing with these, using various coloured inks. She selected one of the quills and started to draw, in red ink, on the top sheet of a pad of paper that was on the desk. I watched for a while - she was very good - and I told her so. I said that I'd like to have a go as well, and stretching out to get one of the quills, my arm brushed the bottle of red ink, which still had the top off it, and sent it flying onto the carpet, where the contents made a large, uneven stain. To say that I was horrified, is putting very mildly - I was panic stricken! Jacqueline though, calmly fetched a wet cloth and tried to remove the stain, but succeeded only in making it worse.   Still remaining quite calm, she said, "oh well, I'll just have to tell daddy that I did it, -- it was an accident after all!" I protested at this generous idea to cover up for me, at the same time as feeling a bit relieved that she had made the offer, and eventually agreeing with her, that it was the most sensible thing to do under the circumstances. I heard no more of this matter, but my punishment for this clumsiness was self inflicted, and for the next several days

I half expected to hear a knock on the door, which - similar to the window incident with the Hodgkins - would lead to my future pocket money being substantually reduced until an expensive cleaning bill had been paid for!

On another day, during those days of impromptu celebration fireworks displays, I constructed a homemade 'smokebomb' from a large roll of film I found discarded in one of the empty houses, after the Canadians had left. I wrapped this up very tightly in some old newspaper, and with Janine and Peter looking on, I set fire to it. The ensuing smoke screen was quite amazing and with the assistance of a light northerly wind, it quickly spread over the Eastern Road - even stopping the traffic for a while, during which time we made ourselves scarce by climbing 'our tree' and staying hidden there until the motorists had eventually left the scene; - this was after one of them had found the offending 'firework,' and in trying to stamp it out, had set fire to his trousers, and coughing from inhaling the smoke, had quickly left the scene to return to his car. Later on, after I had gone in for my lunch, there was a loud knock on our door. My father answered it, and standing there, was the familiar and very large figure of one of our local policemen. Father knew this man, and got on very well with him. I also knew him. He told my father about the smoke screen going across the Eastern Road, and said he'd like a word with me. I was immediately summoned - and duly appeared in front of the constable.

"Now then young sir," he said in his official sounding voice, "the last time you and I crossed paths was one dark night in the blackout about a couple of years ago, when a ghost suddenly appeared from out of the bushes - and that ghost, on seeing that it was a policeman that it was trying to scare half to death - suddenly discarded the sheet it was wearing and ran straight into this house! Now - that wasn't very clever then, and lighting up some sort of a smoke bomb so that it brings the traffic to a halt and throws the whole town into chaos - isn't very clever either, is it? I have it from a reliable source that 'you' could be the red headed young

178

gentleman who is trying to immobilise the country!" I owned up of course; nervous at what my punishment might be at the same time as trying not to laugh at his intentionally funny and overloaded sarcasm. I got away with a ticking off - after promising it wouldn't happen again. After he'd gone, I got another ticking off from my father, who none the less, had found the episode highly amusingly.

Although school carried on after all the celebrations, more or less as normal, a piece of news from the school govenors was that, hopefully, before the year was out, the junior school would move across the road to where the Deaf and Dumb school used to be, and Bristol House would reopen as a boarding house in the senior school.

During that summer the country went to the polls, but just before the real thing - and on a fine day, the junior school held it's own election on the college sports field, with the fives courts being the place where we queued up to cast our votes. Before we went to the vote though, there were some quite enthusiatic speeches made by some of the boys representing the parties involved. The eventual outcome however was different to the outcome of the actual election, because on this day the conservatives came out best! After Labour had been elected in the nationwide ballot, my father, like many of his friends and acquaintances, was very surprised by the result, but said, lightheartedly - "well, at least the new prime minister, Mr. Atlee, should have plenty of common sense - he went to the same public school as me - Haileybury!"

On the warmest days of that summer, with the beaches having officially reopened on July 15th, we went swimmimg a lot - mainly usung the beaches near the Banjo Groyne - where most of our friends used to congregate.

On breaking up for the summer holidays, it was decided that we wouldn't go to Surrey again that year. My mother was still having bouts of sickness and told us she couldn't face any travel or

179

upheaval at all, and in any case - with the hostilities over in Europe - we were alright where we were.

At the beginning of August, on a very warm and humid day, with hardly any breeze at all, my mother, sister and I, each carrying two prawning nets, made our way down to the beaches just near the Black Rock bathing pool, in order to prawn around the railway rocks between there and Ovingdean Gap. It was the first time we had done this since before the war, when we sometimes used to go as far as Rottingdean. These rocks had been laid in the 1890's as an extention to Volks Railway. A special train called 'Pioneer' used to travel from the Banjo Groyne to a pier at Rottingdean, which was where it terminated. In the days that Rudyard Kipling, a keen fisherman, lived at Rottingdean, he could be seen, from time to time, fishing from that pier, and I remember my father saying to me - "It would have been an interesting few hours fishing in the company of that gentleman!"

The train nicknamed 'Daddy Long Legs' - because of the stilt like piles some of the track had to be laid on - included in a long list of famous people who travelled on it - H.R.H.The Prince of Wales, who used it twice in 1898. In 1901 it was closed down and the tracks were removed to make way for the building of new breakwaters - by order of the council. The 'Pioneer' remained moored at the request stop jetty, which had been specially built at Ovingdean Gap, until 1910, when both that jetty and the pier at Rottingdean were demolished. The 'Pioneer' can still be seen at Brighton museum.

That day, while we were prawning the railway rocks, we used one net each for 'spooning' around the weeds that hung into the water from the rocks, and the other nets we baited with some strong smelling old fish, and placed in likely looking holes that went back under the rocks - leaving them there for three or four minutes while we were spooning - then retrieving them, hopefully with a catch of prawns jumping about in the mesh. We used to do quite well when we went on these outings, especially if the weather was humid. On that day, we returned home very hungry and with quite a good catch. Mother immediately cooked the prawns, and they were eaten with some of 'Little Ma's' home baked bread - covered rather extravagantly in butter from the meagre ration allowed at that time.

Whilst we'd been prawning, my father had been sitting in the top gardens talking to Frank, the quiet, slightly mysterious, man from the 'workhouse'. With the prospect of these men soon having to leave the square, he told my father that, like some of his colleagues, he wished he was staying where he was. He also spoke about his past in more detail than he had done beforehand. He had been born in Brighton, an only child, and had lived with his parents until they both died. He suffered - as was obvious to us all - with extreme shyness; he'd had several breakdowns and been 'institutionalised' twice. There had been several jobs - none of which had lasted long, because, he said, "-- of my inability to mix with people." All this had led to his present situation, and he was now in his mid sixties. He said that his favourite pastime was reading - and went on to rattle off a long list of well known authors that he liked, including several classical writers - his favourite being Charles Dickens, and his favourite book - rather aptly perhaps - 'Oliver Twist'.

When it was time for these men to leave the square, my parents gave 'Dopey' some chocolate, 'Kingy' and a couple of others, some tobacco, and Frank - a brand new copy of 'Oliver Twist.'

On Monday August 6th, the news came through of the dropping of an atomic bomb on Hiroshima in Japan, and three days later, the news of the second one on Nagasaki. The horrific details of the devastation caused on each occasion by this, "ultimate weapon," as it was decribed at the time, is beyond description, and it was thought, at the time, that the only good that could come from being able to unleash such an awesome power, was that it could 'just' be the ultimate deterrent to any future war! It was certainly the 'last straw' as far as the Japanese were concerned, and on Tuesday August 14th, they capitulated, and World War Two was now at an end. On the same day as this, there was some very sad news from much closer to home. During the war, we children had often been told by our parents and people in authority, not to pick up any suspicious looking objects that we might find laying about - literally anywhere. It was quite well known that the Germans, on some of their raids, had dropped 'items' that one might be tempted to pick up on finding them, and these would be booby trapped, and would probably explode when being examined or played with. The only things that any of our crowd ever found during those years, after air raids, were pieces of shrapnel laying about. In 'The Argus' that evening was a report that two boys at Worthing, aged thirteen and fourteen, had found an 'object' near where they lived, and on trying to open it up with a hack-saw - it blew up - killing them both instantly. So, on a day celebrating world peace - the war had immediatly started to throw up it's horrific reminders!

V.J.Day was officially declared for August 15th, and although we did go to the Marcy's flat for another party, our celebrations for this occasion were minimal. V.E.night was still fresh in our minds, and for us, that was the important one.

On a windy day, later in the month, I was given permission to get one of the hammocks from the basement; I wanted to try hanging it from one of the trees in the gardens. It had been well over a year since we had last sheltered there during an air raid, and there was already a 'mustiness' about the place again. I sat for a while in the old arm chair my father used to sit in during the raids, and remembered back to those nights when Jill and I sat there with everyone, or lay in our hammocks listening to all the talk. I remembered the fear during the bombing and the humour at quieter times. I particularly remembered the nights when we had listened to Bruce Belfrage reading the nine o'clock news, and later on, seeing him sheltering with us during some loud and frightening air raids. The memories came flooding back, but snapping myself out of it, I took one of the two hammocks down from where it had been hanging since 1939 and returned upstairs. On Monday September 3rd I met Peter and Michael in the top gardens, -

"where's Janine?" I asked them.

"Dunno" Peter said, "unusual for her not to be here by this time." he added.

We decided to climb 'our tree,' and on reaching half-way I could see that someone was already sitting in my usual place, near the top of the tree. On climbing a bit further - I called up - "hello Jan, how long have you been there, and how did you get that high?"

Janine, smiling triumphantly said - "I've been up here for over twenty minutes, secretly watching you lot, and in reply to second part of your question - I've spent too many years with you lot looking down at me - now it's my turn to look down on you!" Although I was a bit put out because she was sitting on the branch that I usually sat on, I did manage to mumble the words - "good for you." We remained quiet for a while after this - the sea looked temptingly close - after lunch we were all going for an afternoon on the beach, and we looked forward to that.

"My mother says that if women were to rule the world, we'd put all you silly men in their places - and there wouldn't be any more wars! I think she's right - don't you?" Janine said tauntingly. If there was one thing Michael, Peter and I had learned from our parents over the years - it was, "never argue with a woman!" -- so we didn't.

"Do you know what you were doing six years ago to today?" I asked them in general.

"How are we supposed to remember that?" Janine asked.

"Well, I can remember - so I'll remind you." I said. "Six years ago to today was September 3rd, 1939, and on that day we were all here in the gardens when the sirens went, and our mothers came rushing in - all panicking - to take us indoors to shelter; in other words it was the day war broke out!"Six years is a long time for children, but of course they all remembered that day very well. The rest of the morning passed quietly, the afternoon on the beach promised to be enjoyable, and the future looked far removed from that summers day - so long ago.

EPILOGUE.

On the first of November 1945 my mother became very ill-this time seriously enough to be rushed into the Sussex County Hospital in the middle of the night. After a few days, the doctors, who couldn't agree on an 'absolute diagnosis,' decided to do an exploratory operation; she never recovered from this, and on November 11th. - Armistice Day - she died. It seemed strange that she should die on the very day set aside for remembering the war dead.

It was decided that it would be best if I didn't go to the funeral - and so on a dull and drizzly day, I watched from the top gardens as the funeral cortege left from Sussex Square for the church of St.Wulfran's at Ovingdean - the place she loved so dearly in life, had now become her final resting place.

We spent a quiet Christmas Day that year with Uncle Charles and Aunt Daphne at their house in Cumberland Road. In February, Daphne gave birth to a boy - Paul.

On a bright day just after Christmas I slipped away from home and made my way over the downs; walking the same paths as I used to with my mother - until I arrived at the church at Ovingdean. I spent just ten minutes alone beside her grave. There were no tears - just a few quiet moments together, with the whispered promise that I would come again from time to time. I still do.

The Lake Superior Regiment returned to Sussex on November 10th 1943 after some very vigorous training exercises in Norfolk.

They were stationed this time at Borde Hill near Haywards Heath. They spent the rest of the winter there; including their

184

second Christmas in England. They trained hard in order to attain a high standard before eventually going into battle. Early in April they moved to Passingworth Park, just near Uckfield, and in the early hours of July 19th., six weeks after D-Day, they started their journey, in convoy, to the docks at Tilbury to embark for the continent, passing through Tunbridge Wells and Sevenoaks on their way. On the morning of the 26th., they disembarked at Red Beach, near Graye-sur-mer in France. The regiment fought it's way into Germany and then back to Holland, where some 'pockets' of Germans still held out. They had distinguished themselves well. The journey back to the 'rocky shores' of Lake Superior began at Nijmogen on 9th. of December 1945. The journey took them into Belgium to embark from the dirty and battered port of Ostend for Folkstone, and then to the Canadian repatriation depot at Aldershot. After all the routine details had been dealt with, leaves were granted for both officers and men, who promptly left off for various places in England and Scotland, where they would spend Christmas with friends and loved ones, before making the final leg of the journey back to Canada. 'Blackie' and 'Mack' arrived on our doorstep just before that Christmas, and at the Rock Inn - "a couple of highly interesting hours passed all too quickly," my father told Jill and me. On the 21st. of January 1946 they set sail on the 'Ile de France' for the home shores of Canada, and on 3oth, at Port Arthur, the Lake Superior Regiment came home to a tumultuous welcome from 'seemingly' the whole population of the area that's now called 'Thunder Bay'.

Peter Margand became a doctor and now lives in America. Janine, who recently had an exhibition of her paintings, lives in Devon. I have no idea where Michael is - nor can I discover the whereabouts of Timmy - I still think of them.

My father, after a lonely year and a half, married Sylvia Chalmers; our very good friend and the lady who used to push me

185

around the gardens in my pram so many years beforehand. She had become a very close friend of my mother's. Sylvia became a mother to my sister and me and managed to hold the family together during some difficult times. Now approaching ninety, she lives in Oxford, and as an ardent Quaker, she still gets about the 'City of Dreaming Spires' and places further afield, and still visits us at least once a year. A remarkable lady, much loved by my sister and me, she is very much involved with both families.

Her brother Alec; my godfather, also lives in Oxfordshire. He recovered well enough from a war injury to eventually go back to teaching. He was awarded the military cross - and later - after retiring as Lt.Col.Royal Gloucestershire Regiment, T.D. - the O.B.E.

Jill became the beauty queen of Brighton in 1947 - one of the prizes for this was a walk on part in Brighton Rock, which was filmed in Brighton during that year. She married Johnnie Silverside a top photographer with the News Chronicle in 1951. After a long and happy marriage Johnnie passed away in 1996 - much missed now by Jill and the son and daughter of the marriage, Jonathan and Joanna. Jill spent quite some years working for Thames T.V. as a costume designer. During her time at Teddington Studios, she and a colleague, Jane Robinson, won 'Emmy' awards for their designs for 'Jenny' - the Thames TV production about Lady Randolph Churchill.

My wife Pamela and I live in the historical city of Rochester. Our three sons Paul, Mark and Timothy have all married. In March 1997, Kerry, the daughter of Tim and Lucy was born - our first grandchild. Animals play an important part in our lives, and, as I write this, Blackie the cat, enjoys some winter sunshine in the garden, while George, the mongrel, with quite a lot of Border Collie about him, sleeps contentedly beside me. Pamela and I have visited Sussex Square several times recently - the gardens are as beautiful as ever. Unfortunately 'our tree' and all but one of the fir trees (Monterey Cypress) were casualties of the great storm in 1987; some of these had to be felled later on - too dangerous to be left standing. The one that does remain in the top gardens, is now 'propped up'. Only a stump remains of 'our tree' with new life growing all around it. I like to imagine that trees have souls, and that like the spirits of those we have loved - they still linger somewhere in the mists of time.

THE AUTHOR

After leaving Lancing College, David Knowles worked for P.A.and Reuters in Fleet Street before joining the regular R.A.F.   Later, as a civilian, he tried his hand in catering; then professional inshore fishing; eventually though, after buying a house in Rochester he went into fruit farming as a Fruit Factor.   He lives with his wife Pamela; the three sons of the marriage are now all married themselves.   His life is now centred around his family including "our first grandchild - Kerry."   Animals now play a large part in their lives, and writing about them and the environment is more than just a hobby.   He has also just started his own 'very small' publishing business which will specialise in hitherto untold true stories of world war two or similar.

The author at Ovingdean, making friends with an inquisitive horse!